THE ACADEMIC REBELLION
IN THE UNITED STATES

Bettina **THE**
Aptheker **ACADEMIC**
REBELLION
IN THE
UNITED
STATES

Introduction by Angela Y. Davis

THE CITADEL PRESS   SECAUCUS, NEW JERSEY

First edition

Published by Citadel Press, Inc.
A subsidiary of Lyle Stuart, Inc.
120 Enterprise Ave., Secaucus, N.J. 07094
In Canada: George J. McLeod Limited
73 Bathurst St., Toronto 2B, Ontario
Manufactured in the United States of America
Library of Congress catalog card number: 72–85518

ISBN 0–8065–0288–6

For Joshua

Acknowledgments

I am extremely grateful to many people who made it possible for me to produce this book. To Jessica Treuhaft, Christian Bay, Albert J. Lima, Gil Green, Susan Castro, Robert Kaufman; to my parents, Herbert and Fay Aptheker; and to my husband, Jack Kurzweil, I express my appreciation for the many valuable criticisms and suggestions. All served as well as a steady source of encouragement and support.

I also wish to thank the Louis M. Rabinowitz Foundation for its generous assistance; Judith Shinn, for her cheerful typing of several versions of the manuscript; Ella Breitman for her special assistance which made it possible for me to do the necessary work.

To Lucy Johns I express my deepest appreciation for her invaluable criticisms of the manuscript from the earliest stages of its inception. She remained as a steady source of encouragement without which this book could not have been written.

To Angela Y. Davis I express my appreciation for her many helpful criticisms, and for the introduction, which she prepared under the most difficult conditions and after more than fifteen months in virtual solitary confinement. It is my first hope that by the time this book is in print, my comrade will be free.

B.A.

January 1972
San Jose, California

CONTENTS

INTRODUCTION

Traditionally, students—and academia in general—have quite naturally found their way into movements demanding progressive social change. Historically, as in the French Revolution and the Bolshevik Revolution a century later, they have made important contributions to revolutions in motion. In this sense, the contemporary academic rebellion has antecedents throughout history, wherever there have been institutions of organized inquiry into human truths. Because students and intellectuals are concerned with articulating and criticizing existing social values, many have often assumed a critical posture vis-à-vis the status quo and its attendant ideology. The continuum of student and intellectual ferment during disparate historical eras and throughout the world may be seen as an expression of this dynamic. Traditionally too, however, "academic" revolts have tended to emphasize absolute moral imperatives and have often reflected an overly intellectualized, contemplative view of concrete political realities.

The precise place of academia in the revolutionary process has long been a question in dispute. During the past decade, virtually every country which has entered stages of advanced capitalism has experienced explosive revolts within and around its institutions of higher learning. Because colleges and universities have been an arena of intense and sustained political activity, a systematic theoretical exploration of the academic revolt has become particularly urgent. Even today, when there appears to be a lull on the campuses in the traditionally defined forms of protest, the growing disaffection from the established order is still manifested in myriad ways.

In her illuminating inquiry into the academic revolt in the United States, Bettina Aptheker poses the following as her central theoretical problem:

Since the advent of the modern protests a single issue has animated all sections of the Marxist movement: Is this rebellion merely an intense version of traditional forms of academic dissent; or does it reflect the beginnings of a qualitative change in the class position of the intellectuals as a whole?

Her affirmative response to the latter proposition forms the heart of her analysis.

Bettina Aptheker is more than amply equipped to explore the implications of this academic rebellion. Having played, as a student and as a Communist, a major role in the Free Speech Movement at the Berkeley campus of the University of California in 1964, she had a part in determining the direction of the campus revolt. She is therefore in a position to base her incisive theoretical analysis on a phenomenon in which she was at one time intimately involved.

The Free Speech Movement, emerging as it did out of the Civil Rights era of the Black Liberation Movement, provides Aptheker with a perspective which, in general, is conspicuously absent from other analyses of the academic revolt. Namely, she places the Black student movement and the broader Black Liberation Movement at the very core of student radicalism. She does not see the Black student movement merely as a separate current within the academic rebellion, but rather also as an organic component of the student movement. She argues that the contemporary student movement has its origins in the reaction and resistance to racism in the United States. One of her essential themes, therefore, is that: "Precisely because the academic rebellion has been intertwined with the Black Liberation Movement and has, at times, been led by Black students, it has significantly altered the fabric of American politics . . ."

Within this framework, the roots of the modern campus protests may be found in the sit-in demonstrations of Black students in the South—specifically, the first sit-ins in Greensboro, North Carolina in 1960. Indeed, the impetus for the Free Speech Movement came from civil rights demonstrations conducted in the San Francisco Bay Area in the Spring of 1964. At that time, students—especially from the Berkeley campus—participated in sit-in actions directed against the hotel industry in San Francisco because of their discriminatory hiring practices. In order to prevent such activities from continuing, the Regents of the University of California instituted a ban on all on-campus forms of political activity. This edict precipitated four months of rebellion during the Fall of 1964, a rebellion for which Bettina Aptheker emerged as a leading spokeswoman.

During the era of the Civil Rights struggle, students—Black and white—left the campus for the wider community. The second half of the sixties saw new offensives emerging from the campus community and specifically directed against the schools themselves. The groundwork for a new political consciousness on the campuses was forged.

The creation of Black and Brown student organizations marked a period of attack upon the racist foundations of the university. Mounting pressure was exerted on higher educational institutions in order to force them to respond to demands for knowledge arising out of the ghettos and barrios. These demands not only called for traditional modes of knowledge but, more significantly, for modes of knowledge which would assist in the development of a militant Black and Brown Liberation Movement. My own experiences at the University of California at San Diego, where Chicano and Black sisters and brothers struggled over a long period of time to establish the Lumumba-Zapata College confirm this view of the intrinsic ties between Black and Brown students and their oppressed communities.

Not only have Black and Brown student struggles reflected community needs and demands; the communities themselves have responded to the demands of Black and Brown students and faculty. During the strike of the Third World Liberation Front at San Francisco State College commencing in November, 1968, the Black, Brown and Asian communities expressed their solidarity with their embattled sisters and brothers by their physical presence on the campus. Prominent leaders from these communities came repeatedly to San Francisco State College and many were arrested.

Dr. Carleton Goodlett, publisher of the largest Black newspaper in San Francisco, led an "illegal" rally on the campus, proclaiming that "The Black community is not going to permit Black students to be isolated on this campus."[1] A Black sociologist on the campus informed the press that

The Black students have captured the imagination of the entire Black community, and we have no choice but to support them. . . . From now on, the governor, the trustees, Mayor [Joseph] Alioto [of San Francisco] and [S. I.] Hayakawa [President of San Francisco State College] will be arrayed against not only militant students and discontented faculty but against the aroused Black community as well.[2]

This interrelationship between the academic revolt and the

Black Liberation Movement is an essential dimension of the historical perspective with which the student movement as a whole must be evaluated. For while Black students and faculty have recently entered the colleges and universities in un-precedented numbers and while the Black Liberation Move-ment has emerged in a new way over the last several years, historically Black people have influenced and have been a part of higher learning for more than a century. Thus, for example, the first sit-in on a college campus was conducted in 1834 at Oberlin College in Ohio. This sit-in was led by the white abolitionist, Theodore Weld, and its central and successful demand called for the admission of Black students.

During the 1920's a significant Black student movement was generated. "Negro students in the Black liberal arts col-leges had rejected the accommodation philosophy of Booker T. Washington and had opted instead for the militant stance of the NAACP leaders . . ." [3] —in particular, W. E. B. Du Bois. In this period, many Black students and faculty members expressed their racial awareness and pride and refused to go along with the white paternalism which domi-nated the white-run Black colleges. Black colleges and uni-versities were (and many still are) under the control of and entirely dependent upon white industrialists and financiers for their survival. The Black poet Claude McKay decried, in the 1920's, ". . . the semi-military, machine-like existence . . ." [4] of Tuskegee Institute. Others, in this same period, denounced ". . . the eternal catering to Southern white sentiment" and said that, typically, the Negro college ". . . is more of a medieval monastery than a modern progressive institution of academic freedom and initiative." [5]

In 1926, when Tuskegee and Hampton Institutes received new endowments totalling $5 million, W. E. B. Du Bois insisted that the administration might now ". . . stop running

your schools as if they were primarily for the benefit of
Southern whites and not for Blacks." He urged that the heavily
endowed administrators

say frankly to all comers . . . this school is not a sanitorium for
white teachers or a restaurant and concert hall for white trustees
and their friends. Those who wish to visit us are more than wel-
come but they must expect to be treated as we treat ourselves.
Our aim is to make Negroes men—nothing less. Those who do not
agree with us though they be old teachers, "best friends" of the
Negro or what not, must stand aside. We are going ahead to
full-fledged colleges of A grade and no longer pretend that we are
simply educating farm hands and servants.[6]

One year after Du Bois' plea, the students at Hampton
Institute in Virginia went on strike. The strike was triggered
by a series of incidents, one of which involved the refusal of
Black students to participate in the "singing of plantation
songs," a feature of the Sunday evening chapel service. On
that particular Sunday (October 9, 1927), the plantation
song concert was an event specially organized for the enjoy-
ment of Sir Gordon Guggisberg, Governor of the Gold Coast.
The strike demands reflected the desire for an end to paternalistic treatment, an end to what Du Bois had described as
"the Negro college as a concert hall for white trustees."
Interwoven with these demands were others which pertained
to the upgrading of the educational program. The strike was
not broken until the administration succeeded in closing down
the school and then expelling four leading members of the
Protest Committee for "insubordination, inciting others to
insubordination and being unsatisfactory in spirit and
attitude." [7]

The struggles of Black students decades ago are decisively
linked to the contemporary protests. Whether white students
fully appreciate the historical precedents for their own protests, or the protests of their Black and Brown contemporaries,

this movement has had a profound impact on the academic revolt. The radical, indeed revolutionary potential of Black Studies—and of Third World Studies in general—entails a new history, a new sociology, a new political science and ultimately even a new perspective for the natural sciences. All this incorporates the experiences of racially and nationally oppressed people which were hitherto unknown to the white intelligentsia in the United States. It has forced many white scholars to develop a new consciousness, however limited, of Black and Brown history and culture and their impact on the history of the United States and the lives of American people.

Moreover, and more fundamentally, as the white students and academics developed a consciousness of the war in Indo-China, and as that protest swept campus after campus, the anti-imperialist consciousness inherent in the Black and Brown experiences penetrated the ranks of the white rebels. It should be recalled that very early in its own development during the Civil Rights era, the Student Non-Violent Co-ordinating Committee aggressively opposed the war in Vietnam and made this opposition an integral element of their program for fighting racism in the United States.

The emergence of an anti-imperialist consciousness among the intelligentsia is immediately attributable to the *combination* of their moral outrage against the war and the new Black consciousness, the new Brown consciousness, engulfing their institutions. As the anti-war movement and the movement against racism and repression mingled and converged, the white component was forced to deal more concretely and more realistically with the nature of American society—and with the concrete needs of nationally oppressed communities and the working class as a whole. Consequently, the late sixties saw a new awareness in the student and academic movement and the consolidation of a conscious Marxist component.

Bettina Aptheker seeks to demonstrate that this new consciousness, derived from the interpenetration of social movements, was reinforced by the new social conditions prevailing
in the university and the new relationship of the university
to the society as a whole.

As a Marxist, Aptheker situates the campus movement
within the broader political movements in the United States,
while seeking to uncover its specific features and its potential
as a distinct thrust originating with students and professors.
This new thrust, she contends, is unprecedented, both in its
politics and in its immediate and long-range objectives. Students and intellectuals in general have participated in virtually
every revolutionary struggle history has witnessed. And in
the United States, political movements have generally rever-
berated onto the campuses. However, the movement climaxed
by the 1970 nationwide campus strike against the war in
Indo-China and racial oppression and repression had qualitatively different foundations and has projected qualitatively
different goals. The key to Aptheker's analysis is that she
detects behind this movement not only a developing political
consciousness among the intelligentsia, but more important,
changing trends in the concrete existence of this group.

Her analysis of the academic rebellion is a penetrating one—
it reaches from the immediately apparent discontent and
disaffection of the intelligentsia down to the material basis
for such reactions. It is not simply that the intellectuals, like
other strata of U.S. society, are becoming increasingly dis-
illusioned. They are of course confronting the dilemma of an
unprecedented technological capacity of the country to solve
the material problems of all its people and the utilization of
this technology in the service of war and profit-yielding enterprises, no matter how contradictory these may be to human
needs. But taking all this into consideration, the more funda-

mental development is that intellectuals are being compelled by scientific and technological progress to become an essential part of the productive process itself.

The core of Aptheker's analysis is a refreshingly new proposition as to how the revolution which has occurred in the production process—in Marxian terms, the base of society—has necessarily given rise to a shift in the class position of the intelligentsia. She argues that intellectuals are now becoming structurally a part of the working class. This revolution in the production process has been generated by and can be defined as the transformation from mechanization to automation. The factory can no longer be seen as the locus of the entire process of production. The universities, too, in which the study of the natural and social sciences is organized and systematized, becomes an essential part of the production process under the impact of automation and cybernetics.

It is this objective process, Aptheker maintains, which lays the material basis for the shift in the class position of the intellectuals, and thus creates and reinforces a new social consciousness through which the intellectuals may embrace the revolutionary and national liberation movements in hitherto unprecedented numbers. The working class has not been replaced, nor has its proletarian core been eliminated. On the contrary, its constituency has been expanded, immeasurably adding to its political power and revolutionary potential.

Bettina Aptheker has written a provocative and extremely important analysis. She synthesizes the actual events of the day, uncovers the social forces which have produced them, and determines how these very same forces have been at work in the ideological-intellectual realm. The academic rebellion, which at first appears to be a contradiction in terms —for the Western intellectual tradition has long been plagued with the separation between things mental and things physical —is placed before us in a new and valuable way.

ANGELA Y. DAVIS

San Jose, California
March, 1972

NOTES

1. Kay Boyle, *The Long Walk at San Francisco State,* New York, Grove Press: 1970, p. 51.

2. *Ibid.,* pp. 51–52.

3. Robert H. Brisbane, *The Black Vanguard, Origins of the Negro Social Revolution 1900–1960,* Judson Press, Valley Forge, Pennsylvania: 1970, p. 101.

4. Herbert Aptheker, *Afro-American History, The Modern Era,* Citadel Press, New York: 1971, p. 179.

5. *Ibid.,* p. 179.

6. W. E. B. Du Bois, "Opinion," *The Crisis,* XXI, March, 1926, p. 216.

7. Edward K. Graham, "The Hampton Institute Strike of 1927," *The American Scholar,* Autumn, 1969, Vol. 38, No. 4, p. 675.

1 THE CRISIS IN HIGHER LEARNING

The first nationwide *political* strike in the history of the United States began on May Day, 1970. It paralyzed the education industry and generated an extraordinary crisis in the country.

There was no national union to organize this strike. It had no nationally recognized leaders. There was nothing to be "negotiated"; and there was no "settlement." Its slogan was thoroughly unorthodox: "On Strike, *Open It Up!*" It was, in inspiration and form, a movement of hundreds of thousands of students and many thousands of professors to "reconstitute" the university that it might begin to "serve the people."

Triggered by the U.S. incursion into Cambodia, the strike was nevertheless organized around three demands:

1) That the United States government end its systematic repression of political dissidents and release all political prisoners, such as Bobby Seale and other members of the Black Panther Party;

2) That the United States government cease its expansion of the Vietnam war into Laos and Cambodia; that it unilaterally and immediately withdraw all forces from Southeast Asia;

3) That the universities end their complicity with the U.S. war machine by an immediate end to defense research, ROTC, counter-insurgency research and all other such programs.

Anyone engaged in the actual politics of the strike knows that it was fraught with difficulties. There was a tendency on the part of many white students and professors to scuttle the issue of racism despite its programmatic prominence. There was dissension between "moderates" and "radicals" over tactics; and repeated evidence of the strategic uncertainty that has long plagued the movement. Still, the overwhelming sentiment was to push these differences aside, to forge a united effort, and to keep the movement going.

Whatever its limitations and ambiguities, the strike demonstrated two incontrovertible facts: the depth of intellectual discontent and disaffection; and the political power of the intelligentsia in advanced industrial society. The May events were the culmination of a decade of intellectual ferment and campus insurgency, intertwined with and responsive to an intense drive for Black liberation.

The academic rebellion is without precedent in the history of the United States. Precisely because it has been intertwined with the Black liberation movement and has, at times, been led by Black students, it has significantly altered the fabric of American politics. It has sparked dozens of different protests all across the country. As it spreads it engulfs every category of institution, from the Ivy Leaguers to the junior colleges. In its wake it unites hundreds of thousands of people of diverse social and ethnic origin. The issues of its concern now reflect serious challenge to the whole organization of society, and its purposes and values. The rebellion marks the rebirth of American radicalism; and this Left Renaissance defines the decade of the Sixties.

The early years of the rebellion focused on the most visible manifestations of social injustice. The students had no theoretical explanation for the existence of these inequities. On the contrary, issues were posed as abstract moral imperatives. Racial discrimination was *wrong,* not endemic to the society, or institutionalized, or organically tied to the political economy of U.S. capitalism. Injustice was viewed as a temporary and unreasonable aberration. Once brought to public attention it would be quickly righted. In 1960 no one other than the Black students and the Black workers of Mississippi and Alabama contemplated *defeat*. The students' view of society was fixed to the contours of bourgeois political theory—it was the *idealized* kingdom of the bourgeoisie; eternal right would find its realization in bourgeois justice; and equality was reduced to bourgeois equality before the law.[1]

The dynamic of the protest movement itself; that is, the official resistance to it, and the students' growing perception of an all-pervasive and worsening social crisis (and then U.S. escalation of the war in Vietnam in the face of official platitudes about our peaceful intentions) contributed to the students' rapid radicalization. Events at the Berkeley campus of the University of California are a microcosm of what was to become a national pattern of protest.

In most of the material that has been written about the 1964 Free Speech Movement at Berkeley, the student sit-in on December 2 and the arrest of some 800 sit-inners, is generally viewed as the climax of the movement. However, the most significant event occurred after the arrests, at an extraordinary Convocation in the campus' Greek Theater, called by the President of the University, Clark Kerr, for 11 A.M. on Monday, December 7.

The arrests triggered a massive student strike which effectively paralyzed the campus. University President Kerr, in an explicit attempt to deflate the strike, called for the Convocation. A crowd estimated at between 15,000 and 20,000 attended. Mario Savio, the principal spokesman for the FSM, requested permission to address the meeting. It was denied. He then requested permission to make an announcement that the FSM would hold a noon rally in the Sproul Hall plaza to respond to the Administration. Permission was again denied. Savio nonetheless decided to make such an announcement. The Convocation proceeded according to the President's carefully drawn plans.

Kerr made a conciliatory-sounding speech; but he offered no substantive concessions on the issues in the controversy. Still, on the whole, his remarks were well received and it was apparent that he had successfully blurred the points of controversy and blunted the cutting edge of the strike. At its conclusion, and after the meeting had been officially adjourned, Savio strode across the stage to the microphone. Everyone remained seated and waited for him to speak. Campus police suddenly leaped onto the stage. Before Savio could say a word he was dragged (by the throat) from the microphone, while other FSM leaders were wrestled to the floor of the stage by the police. The crowd was stunned; then there was pandemonium.

At that moment the President's speech had been stripped to its real non-conciliatory core, and the vital center in the campus' political spectrum had collapsed. The credibility of the center had been irrevocably shattered. That episode more than any other single event revolutionized the *thinking* of many thousands of students.

In the aftermath of the Free Speech Movement the largest event on the Berkeley campus in the spring of 1965 was a Vietnam Teach-in estimated to have attracted between 10,000 and 15,000 people during its two-day program. The U.S. invasion of the Dominican Republic occurred the same week the teach-in was held. For many thousands of students who had just gone through an intensely political experience, involving direct personal encounters with the police, the events in the Dominican Republic and South Vietnam took on a fresh significance.

Intramural hostilities continued during that spring semester.

They were of considerable importance to administrators and legislators; but they were dwarfed by the students' preoccupation with the war in Vietnam. In fact, in the wake of the Free Speech Movement, and as a direct consequence of that experience, the Berkeley campus emerged as the center of the anti-war movement in the United States for at least a year and a half.

Such a massive upheaval could not be confined to purely political issues (if "political" is narrowly construed). Indeed, the political convulsions had an enormous *educational* impact. For once the politics of the protest had embraced radical concerns and perspectives, the university itself, its organization, its purposes, values, and priorities, *had to be* challenged. One faculty commission studying the crisis-ridden Berkeley campus joined the issues this way:

> One major source of our troubles is found in the uncertainty and skepticism concerning the proper relationship between the university and society. . . . That relationship [used to be] based on the assumption that the existing organization of society not only would allow university graduates to contribute their skills in ways that would be socially useful and personally satisfying, but that the broad goals of society were such as to command general approval. . . . Now, however, they are increasingly critical of the world and the institutions that shape it. . . . Some of the most thoughtful and serious students have come to repudiate many of the social goals and values they are asked to serve in the university. . . . This repudiation could be interpreted as the esthetic posture of traditional collegiate disillusion were it not for the growing belief, by no means confined to students, that contemporary society is afflicted with grave problems that it cannot solve and can only worsen. . . .[2]

The social crisis in the United States is *general* and growing deeper. *Nothing* seems to work any more. Every sphere of social life is in crisis: health, education, transportation, communication, housing, employment. Pollution is severe. Taxes are rising. Unemployment is acute. There is an economic depression in the middle of an inflation. None of these problems are momentary; none are even approaching solution. Tens of thousands of men, women and children, are suffering the effects of severe malnutrition, the denial of decent medical and dental care; they are living in destitution or near destitution. The United States has one of the highest infant mortality rates in the world—ranking 12th or 14th (according to the Department of Health, Education and Welfare). In Detroit's richest community the infant mortality rate in 1967 was 12.1 per 1,000 live births; in the city's poorest section it was 69.1.

In the midst of such horrors the rich continue their gaudy amusements. Thus, the *New York Times* can report, with uncanny sobriety, the marriage of two poodles in Palm Beach, Florida: "Along with its dinner parties and lawn parties, the Palm Beach pet set recently attended a fashionable wedding of its own when two well-connected poodles were joined in matrimony at the poodle boutique . . ." The story goes on to describe in detail the gown and jewels of the bride and the "conservative attire" of the groom. It lists the prominent poodle guests, and concludes: "After the wedding party posed for pictures, everyone retired to the patio for a short reception." [3]

This story conveys the insanity of the moment. For the most significant feature of the present crisis is not the anarchy of capitalist relations of production *per se,* but the fact that it is an anarchy in the midst of affluence. That is, we possess the material basis, the scientific and technical ability, to deal with all—certainly the most acute aspects of—the crises. The president of the Univac Division of the Sperry Rand Corporation posed the contradiction very clearly: "From a purely technical standpoint we know how to produce food for every hungry mouth. . . . We know how to eliminate traffic jams. . . . We know how to build virtually indestructible autos, washing machines, houses and other devices that will last a hundred years or more. We know how to build entire cities which are essentially waterproof. Why do we not do these things? Today it is not economically feasible." [4] That is to say, it is not *profitable*.

In this juxtaposition of productive capability and production-for-profit is to be found "the germ of the whole of the social antagonisms of today: the incompatibility of *socialized* production with *capitalistic* appropriation which manifests itself as the antagonism of proletariat and bourgeoisie." [5] The *private* appropriation of *socially* produced wealth (hence the pauperization of all social programs and necessities) presents itself in a new and particularly striking way to students and intellectuals in the present era. They are aware of the material capabilities of the society in scientific and technical detail. They *know* that scientifically and technically the social problems are solvable; and they can therefore see clearly and *concretely* the inability of the social order to realize its material capabilities in terms of human need. In fact, the maintenance of the social order now positively aggravates all social problems. The faculty commission at Berkeley hit upon this fact, and its impact on the universities:

Racial conflicts have become so intense that conventional solutions seem superficial; the ugliness and squalor of cities seem beyond repair and fit only for the violence that erupts in their streets; the skies are fouled and the land and forests ravaged; above all, the republic seems hopelessly entangled in a nightmare of war with ever-widening circles of suffering, destruction, and cynicism. Faced with this crisis many students express intense dissatisfaction with the university, since it provides much of the knowledge and most of the trained personnel required by the technological, and scientific society . . . many students regard as irrelevant the miscellany of superficial, uncertain choices and professional training that often passes as the curriculum.[6]

In the midst of such a general societal crisis four major

themes reflecting various aspects of the crisis in higher education present themselves: (1) the irrationality of the social order vs. the identity of science and scholarship with reason; (2) the undemocratic and regressive qualities of the society vs. the democratic and radical qualities of science and scholarship; (3) the inhumanity and senility of the social order vs. the essential humanism and vitality of science and scholarship; and (4) the illusion of neutrality in scientific and scholarly work vs. the actuality of partisanship.

The irrational, senile, inhuman and undemocratic qualities of the social order are most profoundly manifested in the racism which permeates all aspects of the society and infects all its institutions. The contradictions in the institutions of higher learning, then, are sharpest for the Black students and scholars. As more and more Black people enter the universities and colleges, the resistance, in general, has become more intensive, innovative, diversified; and may now frequently assume a conscious revolutionary thrust.

Each contradiction interacts with the other three; each is thus made more profound; and therefore the totality of the intellectual crisis is intensified and *generalized*. This general intellectual crisis must be discussed in the context of one overriding and central question:

Since the advent of the modern protests a single issue has animated all sections of the Marxist movement: Is this rebellion merely an intense version of traditional forms of academic dissent; or does it reflect the beginnings of a *qualitative* change in the *class* position of the intellectuals *as a whole?* If there is an affirmative response to the second proposition the whole question of revolution in advanced imperialist society is decisively affected. Further, an affirmative response provides the basis for discerning even more clearly and fully the general crisis in academic life.

There are three main trends in the modern spectrum of Marxist thought on this question. First, there are those who assume that the students and intellectuals remain a constituent part of the bourgeoisie. From this it is concluded that while the academic rebels have played a "progressive" political role, the rebellion itself is a bourgeois or petit-bourgeois movement, and will be confined to that.

Second, there is a trend predicted upon the motion that the students exist *outside of the political economy* of the system. From this the students are posed as the primary revolutionary force in advanced industrial society. Being outside of the political economy they do not encounter the temptation and corruptions of affluence alleged to afflict the traditional sectors of the white working class.

A third proposition argues that while the traditional sectors of the white working class can no longer be considered a significant revolutionary force, the students are a prime revolutionary force—not because they are outside of the political economy of the system; but precisely because, for the first time, they are inside the political economy by virtue of the technological revolution.

This book is a contribution toward the further development of Marxist theory, which, in its theoretical conclusions, offers a fourth alternative in its view of the academic rebellion. We affirm the central Marxist proposition that the working class is, by virtue of its position in the productive process, the primary agent of revolution in capitalist society. However, we also affirm that there has been a revolution in the modes of production—a result of the revolution in science and technology—which is altering the *structure* of the working class in advanced industrial society. Further, this revolution in science and technology is causing the production process (known in Marxist terms as the *base* of society) to interpenetrate with the social institutions (known in Marxist terms as the *superstructure* of society) in a qualitatively new way. As a consequence of *both aspects* of this revolution in the modes of production the intellectuals *as a whole* now emerge as a *constituent part of the working class.* This is an *objective* fact which occurs *independent* of the (subjective) ideological or political conceptions of an intellectual or group of intellectuals at any given time. Further, the emergence of the intellectuals as a constituent part of the working class is a *process* now unfolding. This historical moment, then, is to be described as the *process of transition* during which time the position of the entire intelligentsia vis-à-vis the production process is being transformed. It is this process of transformation which at once explains the intensity of the modern protests in higher education, and defines the new relationship of the intelligentsia to the revolutionary process.

Despite its international scope my intent is to deal specifically with the rebellion in the United States. Here it has certain unique features derived from the particular history of the country (especially the institutionalized racial and national oppression of Indian, Black, Chicano, and Asian peoples); the advanced state of U.S. science and technology; its present level of industrial organization and its accumulation of enormous capital resources. In short, the U.S. is the most advanced of the imperialist countries and the complex of forces that have given rise to the academic rebellion reflect, most especially, that fact.

In the classical Marxist view the intellectuals are considered basically to be a constituent part of the bourgeoisie, though the ambiguities in this position are considered. This conclusion is based upon three decisive considerations: a) the absence of any direct exploitative * relationship of the in-

---

* In Marxist terminology exploitation has a precise meaning: it refers solely to the extraction of surplus value from production workers, by the capitalist who owns the means of production. It is for this reason that Marxists may speak of sections of the population who are oppressed, without necessarily being direct victims of exploitation. Further, while all forms of oppression historically grow out of the exploitative relations of production, the elimination of those exploitative relations does not by itself simultaneously end all forms of oppression.

tellectuals in the productive process; b) the particular social functions of the intelligentsia as the creators and promoters of bourgeois political theory and philosophy; c) the select social origins of the intellectuals, designed to maintain an elite corps of scholars and scientists from the propertied classes.

This view of the intellectuals corresponded to nineteenth and mid-twentieth century social reality. Higher education was a privilege reserved primarily for the *sons* of the rich. (In the United States rich also meant *white*.) "Our educational system," observed Upton Sinclair many years ago, with much truth, "is not a public service, but an instrument of special privilege; its purpose is not to further the welfare of mankind but merely to keep America capitalist . . ." [7]

Within this general theoretical frame the Marxists offered three additional and vital considerations. First, while the educational system is understood to be a weapon of the bourgeoisie, learning itself is viewed positively; hence the demand to democratize education. The poor ought not to be relegated to securing only technical and vocational skills; and science and philosophy need not be the sole property of the rich.

Second, there is an appreciation of intellectual ferment as indicative of deepening social crisis. Lenin, for example, polemicized against a proposal that the Bolsheviks abandon their active involvement in the Russian student movement of 1903, even while he affirmed that, ". . . Thousands and millions of threads tie the student youth with the middle and lower bourgeoisie . . ." [8] But, Lenin continued: "The beginning of a mass student struggle . . . means that new powder has begun to accumulate in the powder-flask, it means that *not only* among the students is the reaction against reaction beginning!" [9]

Third and most important, the Marxist philosophy of *dia-*

lectical materialism, indeed, the theory of socialism itself has its roots in "the philosophical, historical and economic theories elaborated by educated representatives of the propertied classes, by intellectuals." Of course, such intellectuals arrive at the theory of socialism through a struggle against that of capitalism; thus, ". . . the founders of modern scientific socialism, Marx and Engels, themselves belonged to the bourgeois intelligentsia . . ." [10]

This was the cornerstone of Lenin's theoretical certainty that the workers would not *spontaneously* develop a socialist revolutionary consciousness. For Lenin the "spontaneous awakening of the working masses . . . to conscious life and conscious struggle . . ." *and* ". . . a revolutionary youth armed with Social Democratic [Marxist] theory straining towards the workers . . ." [11] were *equally essential.*

Lenin affirms the historic inevitability of socialism from the philosophical view; *therefore* he simultaneously insists upon the *actuality* of the revolution—the need to consciously project and organize it; because:

> . . . Socialism and the class struggle arise side by side and not one out of the other; each arises under different conditions. Modern socialist consciousness can arise only on the basis of profound scientific knowledge. Indeed, modern economic science is as much a condition for socialist production as, say, modern technology, and the proletariat can create neither the one nor the other, no matter how much it may desire to do so; both arise out of the modern social forces. The vehicle of science is not the proletariat, but the *bourgeois intelligentsia:* it was in the minds of individual members of this stratum that modern socialism originated, and it was they who communicated it to the more intellectually developed proletarians, who, in their turn, introduced it into the proletarian class struggle where conditions allow that to be done. Thus, socialist consciousness is something introduced into the proletarian class struggle from without and not something that arose within it spontaneously. [12]

At no time in the development of Marxist theory are the intellectuals *in toto* placed in a tangential or hostile relation to the revolution. On the contrary, the Marxist intelligentsia has always been an essential component of the revolutionary movement. In the classical Marxist view the working class (and especially its proletarian, that is to say its industrial, core) is the agent of the revolution, while individual members of the bourgeois intelligentsia are the originators of the revolutionary theory. There has always been an organizational unity between the revolutionary workers and intellectuals— a corollary to the dialectical interpenetration of theory and practice which is basic to the Marxist philosophy. On the basis of their practical experiences the revolutionary workers and intellectuals are then able to develop the revolutionary theory.

This book seeks to analyze the nature of the changing position of the intelligentsia vis-à-vis the production process. It has a triple significance. First, it means that given the concrete position and experience of intellectuals today, a greater proportion of them (than has been objectively possible in the past) will embrace the Marxist philosophy and develop a revolutionary class consciousness. Second, an intense practical/political/intellectual struggle now engulfs the entire intelligentsia—a struggle between those who come into the general orbit of the Marxist philosophy and Marxist politics (without necessarily becoming fully class conscious or actively joining the revolutionary movement), and those who remain within the orbit of the bourgeoisie. While such a struggle is not new in and of itself, it does have decisively new qualities today. For the tendency will be for an increasing number of intellectuals to come into the general orbit of Marxism, while fewer and fewer remain within the orbit of the bourgeoisie. Further, this intellectual struggle is no longer an abstract philosophical debate. On the contrary its outcome has immediate, visible, concrete results which may affect the lives of millions of people in every corner of the globe. The third consequence of this societal transformation affecting the position of the intelligentsia is that their fate is now organically bound up with the fate of the working class as a whole. Therefore, new, practical forms of struggle must be created to manifest the organic unity which now obtains in life.

2 THE CORPORATE CONTROL OF HIGHER EDUCATION

For more than a century the governing boards of most universities and colleges in the United States have been dominated by the representatives of big business.[1] Further, many institutions, especially the most prestigious, owe their survival to the million-dollar benefactions of financiers and industrialists.[2]

A study of the structure and control of higher education in California as a prototype of the rest of the country,* reveals the perpetuation, even the intensification of this corporate control.

California has sixty-three private senior colleges and universities with a total enrollment of 97,000 students.** In addition, it has a public educational system which is the largest in the western hemisphere. It comprises the California State Colleges with eighteen campuses and 200,000 students;

---

* California has both urban and rural centers; agriculture and industry; public and private institutions and a multi-racial population. It has also been markedly affected by the scientific and technological revolution in that the aerospace and electronics industries are heavily concentrated in the state.
** Unless otherwise indicated all figures are for the 1968–1969 academic year.

the University of California with nine campuses and 94,200 students, and 87 junior colleges with a full- and part-time enrollment exceeding half a million.

These are staggering figures. In 1930 there were six University of California campuses with a total of 25,000 students; seven state colleges with 12,000 students and 16 junior colleges with less than 2,000 students. This phenomenal numerical increase in the last forty years is indicative of the changing class origins of the students. In 1966, for example, 37 percent of California's college students in public institutions came from families with an annual parental income of $8,000 or less (which is an admittedly conservative figure for the annual income of many members of the traditional sectors of the working class).[3]

A study of the corporate control of California higher education reveals that:

1) The governing board members of five institutions effectively dominate the resources and control the policies of higher education in the state, by controlling those institutions with the greatest number of students, the largest endowment funds or the most significant research centers (and therefore the greatest financial assistance from the federal government). These five are the University of California, the California State Colleges, the California Institute of Technology, the University of Southern California, and Stanford University.

2) There are some 130 trustees and regents governing these five institutions.* There are six women. The average age is 60. There is one Black trustee who is also the only labor representative. No other ethnic minorities are represented. There are perhaps three or four trustees or regents

* Statistics are based on the composition of these governing boards for the 1968–1969 academic year.

with an academic background above a bachelor's degree (with the exception of attorneys). Seventy-eight of the trustees or regents enjoy directorships on the boards of leading corporations and banks. Thirteen are attorneys, and virtually all of them are specialists in corporate and real estate law.

3) The corporate and financial entities represented on these boards are the decisive sectors of the California economy: banking, agribusiness, electronics, aerospace, transport, oil and mining. The same corporation may be represented several times on the same board of trustees, or on several different boards of trustees by either the same individual or by several individuals from the same corporate entity.

4) These trustees and regents represent a total of thirty-two industrial corporations, thirty-five electronics, aerospace and defense industries, twelve oil companies, five mining companies and three publishing empires; fourteen corporations in agribusiness, five merchandising firms, two shipping lines, four railroads, seven airlines and one trucking line; twenty banks, fifteen insurance companies, eight utility companies; and they own several millions of acres of irrigated farmland in California, Texas, Arizona, and Hawaii.

The changing structure of U.S. big business, most especially the growth of conglomerates and the multinational corporations, has vastly multiplied the concentration of wealth and power represented on the university boards of trustees. Still, the *actual structure* of the university—i.e., of a governing board with substantial control over the academic and material corpus of the university—has remained substantially untouched for two centuries.

The absence of structural change is a principle source of irritation to both students and faculty. A rigid seventeenth century structure based on the ideal of Absolutism still prevails in many institutions. The monarchical skeleton is then clothed in an enormous superstructure of bureaucracy and high finance. There evolves a grotesque, even burlesque, academic edifice.

This antiquated hierarchy paralyzes the educational development of the institution, snares administrators in absurd bureaucratic quandaries and contributes to a general atmosphere of tension and turmoil. The profound intellectual conservatism and racism—not to mention crass ignorance—of most trustees, and the punitive disciplinary policies many of them pursue with a vengeance, is obviously a source of agitation.[4] The governance of the University of California is a case in point.*

The structure of the University is established by the California State Constitution which provides:

—Creation of a Board of Regents as a public trust with "all powers of organization and government."

—The Board shall consist of eight ex-officio members,** and sixteen members appointed by the Governor for sixteen year terms which are renewable.

—The Regents are to be free of "all political and sectarian influences." The Constitution establishes no other criteria for regents' qualifications, and appointments are left entirely to the discretion of the Governor.

This method of appointment has encouraged gross representative inequities and a preponderance of particular political and sectarian influences.

The University of California has been in existence for 102

* The following section on the University of California Board of Regents is a revised version of an article by the present writer which appeared in the *Nation,* September 7, 1970.
** Ex-officio members are: The Governor, Lieutenant Governor, Speaker of the Assembly, Superintendent of Public Instruction, President of the State Board of Agriculture, the President of the Mechanics Institute (San Francisco), the President of the Alumni Association, and the President of the University.

years. In that time there has never been a Black, Chicano, Latino, Indian, Filipino, Japanese, or Chinese represented on the Board.* During the last 25 years there have been forty-eight different gubernatorial appointments to the Board of Regents. A breakdown of the appointments reveals:

—Four Regents with an academic background above a Bachelor's degree: ** Dr. Howard Naffziger, surgeon; Dr. Frederick W. Roman, writer; Dr. Donald McLaughlin, geologist; and Dr. Glenn W. Campbell, the present director of the Hoover Institution on War, Revolution and Peace at Stanford University, a Reagan appointee.

—Two representatives of organized labor, Cornelius Haggerty of the AFL-CIO Building Trades Council, and Einar O. Mohn of the Teamsters, who finished the last year of Haggerty's appointment.

—Twelve lawyers, all of them specializing in corporate and real estate law.

—Four major newspaper publishers: Mrs. Randolph A. Hearst of that vast publishing empire; Mrs. Dorothy B. Chandler, associated with the *Los Angeles Times;* Edward A. Dickson, who had owned and edited the *Los Angeles Times Express;* and Thomas M. Storke, owner and publisher of the *Santa Barbara News-Press.*

—The other 27 Regents appointed since 1946 are bankers and/or corporation executives.

—There are only three women appointees: Mrs. Elinor Heller, whose late husband Edward Heller was also a Regent, a corporation executive, and on the board of directors of the Wells Fargo Bank; and Mrs. Hearst and Mrs. Chandler.

* In 1970 a Black educator, Wilson Riles, was elected State Superintendent of Public Instruction, and thereby became an ex-officio member of the Board of Regents.
** On April 25, 1970, Governor Reagan appointed Dr. John H. Laurence a regent to fill an unexpired term. Dr. Laurence is presently Director of the Donner Laboratory at UC Berkeley and an expert on radiation medicine and nuclear research.

—The average age of the present Board is 60. Many of the Regents who served during the 1950's had been born in the 1880's. One went back to 1866.

In the course of the last two and a half decades the corporate entities consistently represented on the Board have been the Hearst Corporation, which, in addition to its enormous publishing interests owns large chunks of California real estate; and the Bank of America, the largest commercial bank in the United States, with current assets of $25½ billion, and heavy investments in California agribusiness. During the late forties and through the fifties the Hearst representative was that corporation's attorney, John Francis Neylan. The Bank of America was alternately represented by its founders, either L. M. or A. P. Giannini, and in the early sixties by Jesse Tapp, whose tenure as chairman of the board of the bank coincided with his presidency of the California State Board of Agriculture.

This preponderance of corporate and banking executives of aging vintage suggests a conservative political bent. Regental performance in governing the University confirms that conclusion with a vengeance.

Following the 1964 Free Speech Movement at the Berkeley campus of the University of California, the Regents commissioned a Beverly Hills attorney, Jerome C. Byrne, to investigate its causes. His report, submitted to the Board on May 7, 1965, concluded that:

> The crisis at Berkeley last fall has become known as the free speech controversy. It was that, but more fundamentally it was a crisis in government, caused by the failure of the President and the Regents to develop a governmental structure at once acceptable to the governed and suited to the vastly increased complexity of the University. . . ."

The Regents had allocated $75,000 for the production of the Byrne Report. Its significance was apparent in retrospect.

The Regents refused to authorize its official publication. It appeared in a special supplement to the *Los Angeles Times,* but its recommendations were ignored. Whatever criticisms one may make of the report it represented one of the best critical analyses of the governance of the University yet produced.

The Byrne Report punctured the theory that regental posts are honorary:

> The Regents make decisions in every aspect of University operations, including investments, real estate transactions, architectural plans, landscaping, transfers of funds among budget categories, appointments and salary levels of professors and administrators, new academic programs on various campuses and even student discipline. . . .

Confirming the scope of the powers granted the Regents by the State Constitution, the report suggested that a reasonable interpretation of this provision "was not that they [the Regents] should *be* the government of the University, but that they should *make provision for* the government of the University. . . ."

A basic source of academic aggravation is the persistent intrusion of the Regents into the internal affairs of each campus. One UC faculty commission studying the governance of the University concluded that:

> [A]ctions by the Regents . . . have raised serious threats to the academic freedom of this campus, the effective governance of its affairs, and the personal freedom of its students. . . . These incidents are but the most recent examples of a long series of abuses which make a mockery of the official theory that the Regents serve as a "buffer" between the University and the political pressures emanating from a hostile environment. What may have been intended as a buffer has become a conduit for transmitting pressures dangerous to the continuing integrity of the campus. . . .[5]

The regental posture is almost always hostile to the political thrust of significant sections of students and/or faculty.

In the fall of 1968, Eldridge Cleaver, the Minister of Information of the Black Panther Party, was invited to be one of the guest lecturers for a course on the Berkeley campus—Social Analysis 139X: a study of racism in American society. A bitter controversy ensued in which the Regents refused to authorize academic credit for the course.*

The Cleaver controversy lay dormant until November, 1969, when a faculty law suit was filed, petitioning the court to assign credit to the students who had enrolled in the Cleaver course. The significance of Round Two lies in a Regents' resolution which asserted that because the Regents enjoy *proprietary rights* over the University, all records therein, including those of the faculty, were regental property. They instructed the Academic Senate to make available all records pertaining to the controversy.

The faculty refused. The Senate maintained that its records would be released under court order, and only on the premise that Regents' counsel needed the documents preparatory to the pending litigation. The Chairman of the Academic Freedom Committee of the Berkeley Division of the Academic Senate issued a statement which read in part: "To admit that all senate committee files are University records is to present grave problems to faculty autonomy. If faculty records are subject to control and access by the Board of Regents then the faculty senate and its committees cannot function."

The Regents won their court order—but solely on the ground that the records were needed to prepare a defense. Still, the Regents did not rescind their resolution; nor do they deny its validity. It can be invoked at any time.

The divergence of views between students and faculty, on the one hand, and the Regents on the other, has been typified by their respective reactions to particular events surrounding

* The Regents said they would grant credit for the course if Cleaver lectured only once. Students and faculty insisted on ten lectures by Cleaver, as the course was designed.

racial oppression in the U.S., the war in Southeast Asia, and more generally in their respective opinions concerning the proper relationship between the University and society.

In January, 1967, it was disclosed by the student newspaper at the Berkeley campus that a UC chemistry professor, Melvin Calvin, had been serving on the board of directors of the Dow Chemical Company since 1964. At the time Dow contracted with the US government to manufacture napalm for use in Vietnam. Calvin defended his position in an open letter to the students:

. . . As a weapon is effective, so it will be used, and the resources of the entire nation will be utilized by the Government, on request, or by requisition, to produce those weapons deemed by the military to be most effective in concluding the war . . .[6]

The Regents had no comment on the Calvin ethic; nor did they object to his off-campus associations. Presumably both fell within the purview of normal academic functions.

University scientists and engineers often establish contractual and/or consultative relations with private industry or the government. These arrangements are accepted as a natural and necessary by-product of the scientific-technological revolution. The Regents have actively encouraged and protected them. The University, for example, administers and staffs the entire Livermore complex for the U.S. Atomic Energy Commission.

When, however, analogous relations are established between students and community organizations regental opposition smolders and periodically flames. The students, it is argued, embroil the University in partisan political controversy while it is called upon to maintain an aura of scholarly detachment.

Many students respond that the Regents argument is specious and self-serving. Consulting for Dow Chemical or Gulf Oil (or investing $7.6 million of University funds in Dow

Chemical in 1968), they counter, is every bit as partisan as organizing free breakfasts for school children under the auspices of the Black Panther Party.

In February, 1969, Black, Chicano, Asian, and Indian students struck the Berkeley campus to dramatize their demands for the creation of a College of Ethnic Studies and a Black Studies Department. According to a 1969 California legislative study, Black and Chicano students comprise nearly 19 percent of all high school students in California, but total less than 2 percent of the students on all nine University of California campuses.[7]

The Third World students sought to increase the proportion of Black and Chicano students. In a carefully drawn prospectus they developed an academic program relevant to the Black and Chicano experience in the United States, and responsive to the particular needs of their respective communities.

The Regents responded with stunning ingenuity. They called out police from six separate counties, and the governor called in the National Guard. After weeks of intramural combat the Regents agreed to establish the college—on their terms. They allocated $265,000 for its development. An average social sciences department at the University, such as sociology, spends twice that amount just to pay its full-time professors. Three months after the Third World strike the Regents announced plans to build a ball field and a parking lot and allocated $2.5 million for that project. The field and lot were on the site of "People's Park."

By the time the Regents fired Angela Davis, the first time, from the UCLA Philosophy Department in September, 1969, faculty and student defiance was expected and the ensuing crisis bordered on the routine.

For months the Davis controversy simmered under the suspended animation of conflicting court decisions, the prospect of numerous appeals, and a half-dozen different legal suits against the Regents, or the Philosophy Department, or Miss Davis, or everybody; and a new Regents decision at the end of the 1969–1970 academic year firing Professor Davis again. This time the Regents claimed that her speeches on behalf of the Soledad Brothers and other political prisoners were violative of the Regents' professional standards of conduct for academic personnel.

Despite the legal quagmire and subsequent police allegations that Professor Davis was involved in an abortive revolt by Black prisoners from the Marin County Court House, August 7, 1970, which further obscured the question of her academic status, the political convulsions to result from the regental actions were surely predictable.* For with their order to fire Angela Davis the Regents had again, by a single stroke, joined together the most explosive political and social issues of the decade. The action itself projected the issues of Black liberation, academic freedom, political liberty, and women's rights. Miss Davis herself personified the new spirit of radicalism; and too, she marshalled impressive academic credentials. Sixteen months after the second firing the American Association of University Professors published the report of its Committee investigating the dismissal of Professor Davis. The report concluded that ". . . The Regents of the University of California violated recognized principles of due process in the case of Miss Davis . . ." and that ". . . substantial efforts must be made to re-establish at the University of California the unquestioned sense of academic freedom that is essential to a great university . . ." [8]

The California Regents have been shaken by momentary scandal. In the fall of 1970 a California legislative investigation was proposed to determine whether or not UC ad-

---

* On June 4, 1972, Angela Davis was acquitted of all charges by an all-white jury in San Jose, California.

ministrators acted "illegally" or "unethically" when they set up a foundation, with university funds, through which Regent Edwin Pauley personally netted more than half a million dollars. A year before the Berkeley student newspaper, the *Daily Californian* disclosed (January 16, 1969) that millions of dollars of University funds are invested in corporations owned and directed by members of the Board. The University, for example, invested $3.8 million in the Southern California Edison Company of which Regent Edward Carter is a director; $1.05 million into Western Airlines of which Regent Edwin Pauley is a director; and $2.2 million into Lockheed Aircraft, of which Regent John Canady is a director. The disclosures further impugned the integrity of the Regents, and contributed to growing student distrust and anger.

There is increasing evidence that the Regents' ineptitude extends to the purely academic corpus of the University. Robert Reinhold, writing in the *New York Times* (March 2, 1965) reported the beginnings of a faculty exodus from Berkeley and observed that the "rigid bureaucratic administrative framework" was a serious factor in the decision of many to seek positions elsewhere.

The stifling conformity of these aging bankers is even more apparent in their inablity to realize the University's *educational* priorities. With the adoption of the California Master Plan for Higher Education * the University has undertaken a continuous, if haphazard expansion of its facilities and academic programs. This expansion under the Master Plan included a proposal for full year-round operations and the conversion of the academic year from the semester to the quarter system (or nine-week instead of sixteen-week courses).

By an overwhelming majority, the UC faculty repeatedly opposed this change altogether, or contended that the Uni-

* Adopted by the California State Legislature as the Donahoe Act, 1960.

versity was ill-prepared to institute it immediately. Nevertheless the Regents unilaterally instituted the quarter system in
the fall of 1966.

The crazy-quilt programming of undergraduate education
underwent another dazzling renovation. Frantic efforts were
undertaken to restructure courses, and either cram into nine
weeks what had previously been taught in sixteen weeks, or
cut programs and reschedule them. The entire quarter scheme
proved to be a useless gesture a year later when the Reagan
administration instituted its first budget cuts in University
funds. The present level of state funds barely allows the
University to hold its own, and precludes the possibility of
physical expansion which is the prerequisite for a year-round
operation.

The University of California does continue to function. The
white clouds of tear gas lift over the Berkeley campus and a
semblance of "normality" returns.

Still, the Governor began the 1970–1971 academic year by
calling for the dismissal of two UCLA Law Professors for
"unprofessional conduct." The Santa Barbara campus continues to sizzle, while the *sole* official response of the Regents
to its conflagration in the winter and spring of 1970 was a
new set of disciplinary rules, mandating the Chancellors of
each campus to impose immediate interim suspensions on
any student, employee or faculty member "where there is
reasonable cause to believe he has violated any University
or campus regulation by disruptive acts." This regulation was
not only opposed by students and faculty, but by all nine
University Chancellors in public statements, on grounds that
it limited their flexibility in critical situations. But the Regents
insisted upon its adoption.

Many of the worst crises and confrontations on the University of California campuses have been either provoked directly by the Regents or aggravated by a punitive disciplinary
policy. More importantly, very large numbers of students

have been driven into a fury of agonized frustration over the *unresponsiveness* of the Regents, and higher authorities in general, to their demands, concerns, and aspirations.

Many faculty are now convinced that the state constitutional provisions for the governance of the University require substantive modification, although most hold out little hope that it can be done. In 1965 a California Assemblyman from San Jose, William Stanton, proposed a constitutional amendment which provided that criteria be established for Regents' appointment to guarantee some standard academic qualification, and equitable student, faculty, community, and ethnic representation; that the length of regental service be reduced; that the powers of the Board be specified and delimited. The Stanton amendment died in Committee, but the issue remains very much alive.

The pattern of repeated crisis and the convergence of issues in the Davis controversy is illustrative of the depth of the University's malaise. For while particular injustices have inspired each campus upheaval, the persistence of insurgency, the escalation of confrontation, and now the fusion of issues suggests the degree of structural disorder.

Still the corporate control of the higher educational system is nothing new, and does not in itself explain the scope and intensity of the contemporary rebellion. Indeed, the trustees have been firing radical professors and dismissing "incorrigible" students for at least a hundred years.[9]

The corporate control reflects the particular socio-economic and political functions of the academy. It is precisely here, in the functional realm, that we believe a decisive transformation has occurred which lies at the heart of the contemporary revolt and has simultaneously transformed the relationship of the students and the intellectuals, *as a whole,* to the revolutionary movement.

3 THE REVOLUTION IN SCIENCE AND TECHNOLOGY

Since the end of the Second World War the number of colleges and universities in the United States has almost doubled. The number of matriculated students has increased seven times. The federal government has astronomically increased its financial support of higher education. The corporate elite continues to effectively manage and control the academy. All of this suggests that in the post-war era the university may have assumed certain strategic functions which are essential to the further development of an advanced industrial society.

John Kenneth Galbraith describes one aspect of the new functional quality of the university: "The industrial system, by making trained and educated manpower the decisive factor of production requires a highly developed educational system . . ." [1] Furthermore, since the Second World War there has been a revolutionary change in the instruments of production which has effected a *qualitative* change in the relationship of the university to the production process.

This revolution may be defined as the conversion from mechanization to automation. It replaces manual control in industry with electronic control. It is made possible by and reinforces an inversion in the relationship between science and technology in which scientific progress *precedes* technological capability.

Early technology was the product of invention requiring nothing more than a rudimentary grasp of the laws of nature. Machines could be conceived, designed and constructed on the basis of the most elementary scientific concepts and intuition. Science was only tangential to this process, as Lewis Mumford observed:

> The detailed history of the steam engine, the railroad, the textile mill, the iron ship, could be written without more than passing references to the scientific work of the period. For these devices were made possible largely by the method of empirical practice, by trial and selections; many lives were lost by the explosion of steam-boilers before the safety valve was generally adopted. And although all these inventions would have been the better for science, they came into existence, for the most part, without its direct aid . . .[2]

With the advent of modern industry it became necessary for man to consciously employ his scientific knowledge to develop his technological capabilities. The introduction of machinery in the production process required the "conscious application of science instead of rule of thumb . . ."[3] From its tangential or accidental relevance to technology, scientific discovery was now consciously applied to develop man's technological capabilites.

In this way technological demands became the main motive force for scientific discovery. A classic example of this was the discovery of the laws of thermodynamics, born from a search for the most efficient utilization of the steam engine.[4] "The varied, apparently unconnected and petrified forms of the industrial processes now resolved themselves into so many conscious and systematic applications of natural science to the attainment of given useful effects."[5]

From Mechanization to Automation

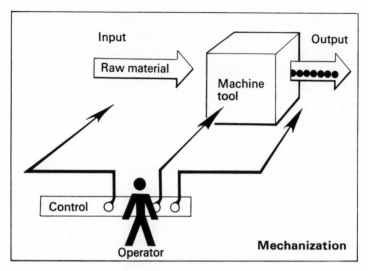

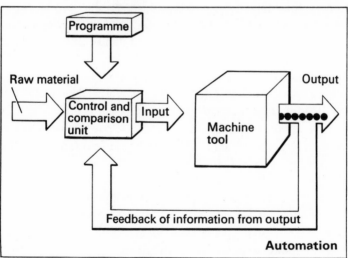

From *The Electronic Revolution* by S. Handel,
Penguin Books, London, 1967

The growing sophistication of technological achievement finally produces a change in the relationship between science and technology. To wit: "Scientific progress becomes the *motive force* for developing technology." [6] That is, scientific progress now *precedes* technology instead of following at its heels. The nature of this change in the relationship between science and technology can better be understood in the context of describing an assemblyline in modern industry before and after automation.

Human labor on the assemblyline before automation is not only the labor of hands. It is also the labor of eyes and brains. As the raw material is transformed into the finished product it is under constant human inspection, and corresponding adjustments in tool settings are made to compensate for a variety of actual or expected margins of error. The essence of automation is that this human element in production is eliminated and replaced by the electronic element. Sensor and effector organs replace not only eyes and hands, but the human brain. The "electronic brain" (a computer) stores information, processes information and communicates necessary information to sensor and effector organs which then make the required adjustments during the production process. In this way the computer acts to direct and control the production process (or parts of it). This is the quintessence of the revolution in the instruments of production.[7]

As the desired complexity of a given industrial process increases there must be a corresponding sophistication in the electronic element. In other words, as the volume of information to be stored, processed, and communicated by the central computer expands, the complexity and speed of that computer must correspondingly advance.

It is this process of correlation between the complexity of the industrial process and sophistication of the electronic component that renders scientific progress the *essential* pre-

Main Units of a Digital Computer

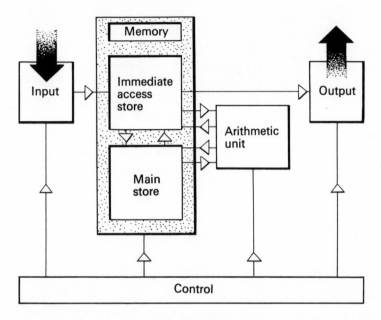

requisite of technological capability. That is, the development of technology is *determined* by the discovery of new scientific or mathematical laws. It is, of course, possible to improve the electronic instrument in a technical, mechanical, or structural way. However, to further develop its ability to process information, or to improve its accuracy and efficiency in the transmission or information, depends *primarily* (although not exclusively) upon scientific or mathematical discovery. The recent development of computers capable of responding directly to verbal commands (as opposed to punch-card or magnetic tape instructions) is a case in point. The ability of the computer to recognize patterns formed by sound frequencies is directly attributable to theoretical achievements in mathematics.

Further, the conversion to automation will ultimately require that the sources of energy, upon which the whole productive process depends, be revolutionized. This will mean the conversion from steam, and the mined fuels such as coal and oil as primary sources of energy, to the fast-breeder fission reactor and/or controlled thermonuclear fusion. Here again, the development of such new energy-sources is primarily a scientific rather than a technical problem.

Any revolution in the instruments of production makes necessary a revolution in the general condition of the social process of production; that is, in the means of communication and transport. This is certainly true today; witness for example the development of containerization in the shipping industry. However—and this is the essential point—the present revolution in the instruments of production—the conversion from manual control to electronic control—may be *defined* as a revolution in the means of communication. *The correlation is simultaneous, causal, and interpenetrating.*

For the essence of control *is* communication. Norbert Weiner explained this concept of control through communication this way:

When I communicate with another person, I impart a message to him, and when he communicates back with me he returns a related message which contains information primarily accessible to him and not to me. *When I control the actions of another person, I communicate a message to him, and although this message is in the imperative mold, the technique of communication does not differ from that of a message of fact.* Furthermore, if my control is to be effective I must take cognizance of any messages from him which may indicate that the order is understood and has been obeyed. [Emphasis added.—B.A.] [8]

The revolutionary quality inherent in the electronic component is not in its ability to process information (that was accomplished albeit in a most primitive and mechanical form by the mathematician Charles Babbage in the 1830's); but in its ability to store or "memorize" information and to select the necessary information to direct and control a productive process.[9]

This communicative revolution in the instruments of

production signals a revolution in the *nature* of communication in human society. Man's capability is revolutionized.
He assumes the scientific and technical potential to direct
and control productive, natural, and social *processes* as distinct from his previous ability which was limited to the *partial*
direction and control of *particular* (and often unconnected)
productive, natural, and social *forces*.

Automation thus provides the material basis for science
itself to emerge as a *direct* productive force. Science may
now penetrate all phases of production. It will gradually become the central productive force of human society.[10] It now
sustains its own dynamic, acting as the motive force for technological change:

> . . . *The perspectives of science* suggest some foreseen, but as
> yet unfathomable potentialities that may revolutionize production
> techniques and man's whole way of life during the next decades:
> application of magnetoplasmo-dynamics effects, quantum gener-
> ators of electromagnetic radiation (lasers and masers), controlled
> mutagenesis, induced changes in the structure of the organism,
> etc. While their practical application will be a relatively long-term
> matter, their existence underlines the deep-lying acceleration trends
> of the scientific and technological revolution.[11]

But at this moment we must *redefine* our concept of the
productive process altogether. It is no longer *enclosed* in the
factory *per se*. Production is no longer synonymous with
"industrial." On the contrary; with science as a direct productive force production must be seen as the *all-inclusive
integration of industrial, natural, and social processes*. It is
for this reason that ". . . automation is not simply an extension
of mechanization . . . automation is a contemporary phenomenon of a revolutionary nature . . ."[12]

Automation signals the birth of a new science of communication: *cybernetics*. The essence of it may be defined as the
conversion from component analysis to systems analysis. In

other words, there is a gradual development of man's capability—from the schematic and partial prognosis of *particular* industrial, natural, and social *forces,* to the systematic and integrated prognosis of *complete* industrial, natural, and social *processes.*

It is to be expected that such a revolution in the nature of the production process would effect deep changes in both the social combination of the labor-process and in the functions of the laborer. That is, as Marx predicted, the creation of real wealth now depends less on the labor-time and on the quantity of physical labor expended, and more on the power of the instruments of production. The effectiveness of these instruments is not related to the labor-time immediately expended in their production, but depends rather on the general state of science and the progress of technology . . .[13] Further, Marx projected a change in the structure of the working class itself. That is, man no longer appears enclosed in the process of production; rather he acts as its supervisor and regulator. He stands *at the side* of the productive process, instead of being its chief actor.[14]

Still, the conversion to automation does not in and of itself change the *social relations of* capitalist production. The private ownership of the means of production is maintained and the private appropriation of socially produced wealth continues. Automation affects the *structure* of the working class; but it does not alter its *exploitative essence.*

To explain this further: when man developed machinery to perform physical labor which he himself could not do, that machinery represented an extension of his *physical* capabilities, and simultaneously revolutionized the production process itself, ushering in the era of Modern Industry. Marx fully appreciated its revolutionary quality:

Modern industry never looks upon and treats the existing form of a process as final. *The technical basis of that industry is there-*

fore revolutionary while all earlier modes of production were essentially conservative. By means of machinery, chemical processes and other methods, it is continually causing changes not only in the technical basis of production, but also in the functions of the labourer, *and in the social combination of the labour-process* . . .[15] [Emphasis added.—B.A.]

Still, the introduction of new machinery did not change the *quality* of the social (and political) relations of capitalist society. It provided the material basis for the consolidation of those relations.

The development of the electronic element represents an extension of man's *mental* capabilities. As we have sought to show, automation is not merely an extension of mechanization. On the contrary, automation revolutionizes the nature of the whole production process. Still, it does not change the social (and political) relations of capitalist society. It provides the material basis for that change; *that is, it lays the technical and material basis for Communism.* But to actually alter the *quality* of social relations requires a *political* revolution.[16]

The conversion to automation does accelerate the entrance of engineers, technicians and scientists into the production process. Marx observed the entrance of scientific workers into industry, but only on a rudimentary level, when as he put it, they were "numerically unimportant." Still, he viewed their division from manual workers in the production process as a "purely technical" one. Likewise, Lenin, in discussing the material and technical basis of Communism, projected the necessity of abolishing the distinction between "manual workers and brain workers." [17]

Today scientists and technical workers comprise a continuously expanding percentage of the total work force. In 1920 there were only 215,000 scientists and engineers in the United States. Two hundred thousand of them were

Scientists and Engineers in the U.S.: 1900-1960.

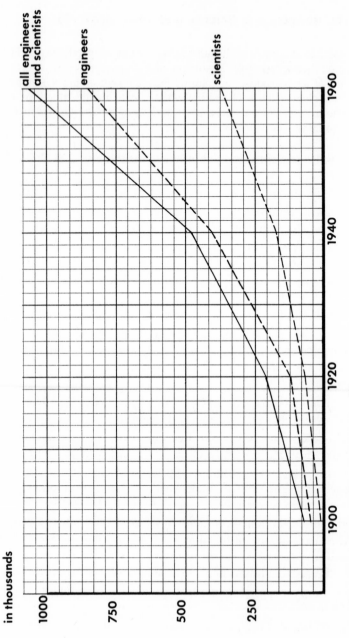

Source: The Technical Elite, Jay M. Gould, p. 172.

employed directly in U.S. industry. That was little more than one half of one percent of the 37 million people employed in all occupations in that year. Even so it represented the largest assemblage of industrial technologists in the world at that time.[18] By 1960 there were one million engineers and scientists employed directly in U.S. industry—a numerical increase of 8½ times.

The tendency of automation is to steadily increase the number of scientific and technical workers engaged in the production process. However, it does not necessarily follow that there is a decrease in the number of manual workers engaged in the production process. On the contrary the number of manual workers so engaged also increases. What may be said is that the *proportion* of scientific and technical workers engaged in the production process tends to increase.*

In addition to this direct employment of scientists and engineers in industry, there are today contractual and/or consultative relations between academicians who work *directly for an industrial complex while remaining physically situated in the academy;* or there are scientists and engineers who glide back and forth across the country employed first in private industry, then in the university. A startling result of the contractual arrangement is that whole departments (or institutes) at one university may suddenly depart and move to another where the financial offers or research facili-

* Further clarification is necessary. The United States Census Bureau deliberately creates absurd categories for so-called white collar workers in an effort to lend statistical credence to the theory that blue-collar (manual) workers are disappearing in the United States. It does this by expanding the so-called white collar category to include mail carriers, telephone workers, supermarket employees, cashiers, etc. Further we emphasize that we are not discussing here all workers, we are specifically discussing production workers. Thus for example our discussion does not encompass all of the workers in the service industries, where manual workers are employed in large numbers. (The growth of the service industries is also, in part, related to automation). See the very important article by Andrew Levison, "The Working-Class Majority," in *The Nation,* December 13, 1971, pp. 626–628.

ties from a competing university (or corporation) are more enticing to the department chairman (or institute director) and his colleagues. We thus have the spectacle of academic entourages traipsing back and forth across the country.

Whether employed directly in industry or in a contractual capacity while remaining physically situated in the university, these intellectuals become production workers in the Marxist sense. For it is not the physical location of their work, their annual income, or their ideological suppositions, but their (objective) relationship to the productive process which *defines* their class position:

Production workers are technically defined by Marxists. Only such labor as takes a direct part in the production of commodities and consequently, in the production of surplus value, is considered productive in a capitalist economy . . . However, the labor of scientists, engineers, research and laboratory workers and their auxiliary clerks and other staffs whose work forms a direct constituent part of the process of production of commodities should be classified as productive workers . . .[19]

With the growing demand for scientists, engineers, and technicians brought on by the conversion to automation the universities and colleges become the centers for training these intellectual workers. Again, Marx observed a similar function of the educational system (but on a more elementary level corresponding to nineteenth century technology). He predicted that as the complexity and variation of the industrial processes advanced, so would the technical capability and versatility of the work force. He suggested that the bourgeoisie, in spite of itself, would be forced by technical necessities, to establish some form of educational program for the working people.[20]

A parallel development took place in the United States during and after the Civil War. The Morrill Land Grant Act of 1862 provided for the establishment of the land grant colleges and the state universities,* to provide technical education in such subjects as agriculture, mining, and engineering.

The analogous contemporary development is the unprecedented expansion of the junior (sometimes called community) colleges.** As one authority explained: "Of all types of higher institutions, the junior colleges have experienced the most rapid growth . . . And if the plans of many states materialize, it will be expected to absorb a large part of the explosive increase in college attendance that lies just ahead . . ." [21]

In June, 1970, the Carnegie Commission on Higher Education issued a marathon report on education in the United States. It recommended as a major priority the rapid expansion of the junior college system during the seventies, to bring one of the two-year schools within easy reach of every student and adult in the nation. According to the report one of the major assets of the community college is that it offers working adults lifetime opportunities for retraining and reeducation to protect themselves against educational and occupational obsolescence.

The junior college student now accounts for more than half the total enrollment in California higher education. State government figures in 1966 indicated that 42.2 percent of the junior college students came from homes where the parental income was less than $8,000 a year, suggesting that very near to a majority of these students are of traditional working-class origin. The priority function of the junior colleges, as defined by the California Master Plan for Higher Education, is: ". . . vocational-technical education and training

* The University of California is a land grant college.
** This phenomenon is most pronounced in the western states. The expansion is more limited east of the Mississippi. The main reason for this is that the basic center for the electronic and aerospace industries which most need technical workers is west of the Mississippi—primarily in California and Texas.

to prepare students for occupations which require two years of training or less . . ." Other studies indicate that the junior colleges also serve as the vehicle to obtain preliminary training prior to seeking admission to the state colleges and private universities.* For example, the Engineering School at Los Angeles State College reported that in the fall of 1967, 80 percent of its juniors and seniors transferred from junior colleges.** [22]

While the presence of technical and scientific workers in the production process is not new, there has been a dramatic increase in their numbers; and corresponding modifications in the higher educational system have been made. Still, this represents only a quantitative change in the relationship of the university to the production process.

The new *quality* in that relationship is to be understood in the context of science becoming a *direct* productive force—providing for the all-inclusive integration of industrial, natural, and social processes. Specifically: the university is the institution in which the study of the physical, natural and social sciences is organized. A central and immediate consequence of the electronic revolution is that the university assumes an *organic* connection to the production process. For as scientific progress precedes technological capability and as science emerges as a direct productive force, the syste-

* Because of both class and racial discrimination in the elementary and high schools the majority of young people from working class families (using an annual parental income of $8,000 to denote working class) do not "qualify" for admission as freshmen to the state colleges, universities, and private institutions. If they attend a junior college and successfully complete two years they are eligible to apply to a four-year school. Whether or not they get in is another matter. In California, 1966 statistics show that 30.6 percent of the students in the state colleges, and 23.3 percent of the students at the University of California, were of working-class families.
** Nationally about one third of the engineering schools report significant junior college transfers (with 5 percent as a threshold of significance). These schools are concentrated west of the Mississippi.

matic, interdisciplinary research, embracing the natural, social and physical sciences, which is most effectively organized within the university, becomes the *essential* prerequisite for technological development. It is this fact which increasingly renders the university, as an institution, a *constituent part* of the productive process.

This change in the relationship between the university and the production process is reflective of the fact that as science becomes a direct productive force there is a tendency toward an organic unity between social institutions and the production process. That is, the economic base of society (the infrastructure) tends to interpenetrate with the superstructure of society in a new way.[23]

The emergence of the university as a constituent part of the productive process is the *material* basis for a qualitative change in the class position of the intelligentsia. That is, it is becoming a constituent part of the working class.

4 THE IDEOLOGICAL FUNCTIONS OF THE UNIVERSITY: MANIPULATION AND CONTROL

The ascendancy of science to a direct productive force has a profound social impact. The Corporate Elite at once attains the technical capability and acquires the political-economic necessity to transform the ideological functions of the university. Traditionally intellectuals have been expected to provide the philosophical and theoretical foundations for the existing social relations, for the *status quo*. The Corporate Elite now seeks to develop the ideological function of the university utilizing it as the instrument through which to manipulate and control internal and international *social* processes.

Once the social order is in general crisis, and many of its institutions are impaired or in danger of actual collapse, a purely theoretical defense of it is hardly adequate. Bourgeois political economy, for example, ". . . throws overboard, most of its purely academic concerns in order to become a technique for the practical consolidation of capitalism . . ." [1] The same tendency appears in political science, the behavioral sciences, sociology, anthropology, psychology, and so forth. The social and behavioral sciences become instruments for developing techniques to control and direct patterns of human behavior. Their fulcrum of attention shifts from the theoretical to the functional realm.

Marxism, of course, insists that purely theoretical contemplation, being passive and non-participating, *cannot* be fully comprehending.[2] But the bourgeois academics have not embraced this Marxist view of theory and practice. On the contrary, they have tended to abandon theoretical reason, and replace it with *operationalism* in the physical sciences and *behaviorism* in the social sciences: ". . . The common feature is a total empiricism in the treatment of concepts; their meaning is restricted to the representation of particular operations and behavior." [3]

Using the concept of length as an example, the physicist P. W. Bridgman explained the essential features of operationalism in this way:

To find the length of an object, we have to perform certain physical operations. The concept of length is therefore fixed when the operations by which length is measured are fixed; *that is, the concept of length involves as much as and nothing more than the set of operations by which length is determined.* We mean by concept nothing more than a set of operations; the concept is synonymous with the corresponding set of operations.[4]

Further, Bridgman insisted upon the *uniqueness* of each set of operations for each concept:

In principle the operations by which length is measured should be uniquely specified. If we have more than one set of operations, we have more than one concept, and strictly speaking there should be a separate name to correspond to each different set of operations.[5]

The principle of conceptual uniqueness (a virtual contradiction in terms) precludes the existence of theoretical reason; that is, it assumes the impossibility of theoretical evaluation and unification. Operationalism, then, is the theory of "non-theory"; just as pragmatism, in a correlative way, is the philosophy of no philosophy.

If all concepts must be synonymous with a particular set of operations, it follows that questions whose answers cannot be operationally derived, are meaningless. Indeed, Bridgman concludes that many social and philosophical questions will be found meaningless when examined from the operational view. And, ". . . just as in the physical domain, so in other domains" Bridgman continues, "one is making a significant statement about his subject in stating that a certain question is meaningless." [6]

Carrying Bridgman's thesis to its logical conclusion, it can be presumed—in fact, it is all too often assumed among social and behavioral scientists—that moral and ethical questions, unconducive as they are to operational solution—are meaningless. The study of contemporary ethics, is, for example, reduced to an absurd exercise in *metaethics:* ". . . an analysis of when and why people might *say* that something is 'good' or 'evil' or that an action is 'right' or 'wrong' . . ." [7] Only in this way, it is argued, is ethics "operational," therefore "meaningful." Operationalism provides its own moral justification by rejecting morality as a "meaningless" concept. Operationalism then appears to be an internally consistent theory. Its method of reasoning is circular and self-contained. For it, non-operational ideas are simply non-existent, or subversive: "The movement of thought is stopped at barriers which appear as the limits of Reason itself." [8]

Operationalism serves as the main theoretical and methodological basis for the social and behavioral sciences in the United States. It is, as Marcuse observed, the "theory and practice of containment." That is, operational theory assumes the functional stability, inevitability, and permanence of the capitalist economic, political, and social structure. It must therefore be exclusively concerned with its functional efficiency, technical proficiency and practical consolidation. Correspondingly, the *social purposes* of scholarship are pre-defined and unchangeable. Literary and historical works may now be extracted from their social contexts lest they present themselves as critical commentaries on contemporary life.

Commenting on the "scandal of literary scholarship," for example, Louis Kampf observes that:

> The profession's very attempts—be it the History of Ideas or the New Criticism—to divert scholarship from its positivist pretentions, from its obsession with mechanical tasks, have themselves become petrified into empty techniques . . . New Criticism, which began as an attempt to force a critical confrontation between reader and poem, has (inevitably, one feels) become a method of avoiding thought about the poem altogether: the student is so busy tallying examples of irony, paradox, tension, and so forth, that he can barely fathom the meaning of the words.[9]

Similarly, an economist comments upon the irrelevance of dominant economic trends to major issues and controversies in American life as it remains preoccupied with quantitative analysis:

> The major innovations of recent years have been in quantitative methods, highly useful for problem-oriented research and for practical use . . . [this] stress on [what may be called] scientism is itself a kind of ideology; it suggests that the central values of the economic tradition in the West—free markets, efficiency, growth—are sufficiently valid for our time to require no further serious scrutiny. Rather they are the accepted base on which to build more effective techniques for achieving them.[10]

Further, of course, as radical economists have suggested, this preoccupation with technical matters produces both a scientific sterility and a highly conservative bias:

> The problems that yield swiftly to the thrust of young and inventive minds are the highly abstract, mathematical models that produce snappy deductions and reams of computer print-outs. Whether the deductions or the computerized correlations and

other estimates have any particular relation to what actually happens in the economic world, or to the deeper question of how to change the world, may be incidental if not irrelevant. The important thing is that they yield "papers," and sometimes even books, and they are so impressive with the inverted matrices and vector spaces that in some instances only their authors, and an associated colleague, can understand them.[11]

Similar technical tendencies prevail as the dominant trends in sociology and political science, where ". . . fundamental patterns of social structure remain obscured. . . . For the quantitative approach rules. Measuring the measurable rather than asking the fundamental questions of content, value, and alternative, becomes the road to a vigorous ordering of evidence . . ." [12] The technification and quantification of the academic disciplines has been an historical tendency in U.S. scholarship; but it prevails today to an unprecedented degree.

At the end of the Second World War the United States emerged as the dominant imperialist power. This occurred simultaneously with the securing of socialism in the USSR, the advent of socialism in Eastern Europe and subsequently in China, Korea, Vietnam, and Cuba; and the shattering of colonial rule, as movements for national liberation erupted everywhere—including within the United States where the movement for Black liberation gained a fresh intensity. The changed position of the United States evoked immediate response. The academy experienced its first adjustments to the new era.

University-affiliated social science research institutes blossomed. Their purpose (at times explicit, at times implicit) was to thwart the movements for national liberation, reverse socialist revolutions where they had already occurred, and develop the philosophical and ideological challenge to Marxism.

An official publication of the U.S. State Department noted

that by the early 1950's "there were few policy-makers [in Washington] who did not see the relevance of social science research in its broadest sense to the new position of the United States in the world . . ." [13]

Even more explicit was a 1960 report prepared by the Committee on University and World Affairs. In discussing the international role of American universities the report said:

> . . . Our basic knowledge of a vast array of foreign societies, of international relations and of economic growth and social change is gravely deficient. If our understanding and our capacity to act in such areas as Asia, Africa and Latin America are to be illuminated by critical appraisal, greatly expanded opportunities are needed for scholarly studies of these countries and United States relations with them . . . [14]

The universities provided the vehicle for the establishment of the international studies institutes. Through the fifties the emphasis of these institutes was on the collection and evaluation of data to provide policy-makers in Washington with reliable information.

The Foreign Policy Institute at the University of Pennsylvania, for example, established in 1955, has as its purpose:

> . . . To examine the fundamental, long-range problem of United States foreign policy, the developments within the Communist world . . . the problems of development in Asia, Africa and Latin America, and the influence of technology on the future political order. [15]

The research Institute for Cuba and the Caribbean at the University of Miami has as its purpose the study of "all aspects of the Cuba situation . . . such as . . . the sources of social tensions and political instability, the sociology of change and varied aspects of the ideological struggle and its consequences . . ." [16]

The Hoover Institution on War, Revolution and Peace at Stanford University was begun in 1919 to gather documents on World War I and twentieth-century European political and economic movements. In 1959 the Institution's functions were radically altered by the 85-year-old former President Herbert Hoover, who authored a new statement of principles:

The purpose of this Institution, must be, by its research and publications, to demonstrate the evils of the doctrines of Karl Marx—whether Communism, Socialism, economic materialism, or atheism—thus to protect the American way of life from such ideologies, their conspiracies, and to reaffirm the validity of the American system.[17]

This institution is financed to the tune of two million dollars annually, through the benefactions of foundations and top executives from such corporations as Standard Oil of New Jersey, Gulf Oil, Mobil Oil, Union Carbide, U.S. Steel Corporation, Republic Steel, and Lockheed Aircraft.

In the early sixties the social and behavioral sciences shifted toward a more direct, operational counter-insurgency. From the relatively passive computation and evaluation of data the behavioralists and social scientists now moved to active intervention in the internal affairs of other countries, seeking to manipulate behavioral patterns under the guise of "field studies" for apparently legitimate research. The goal was to develop political, social and/or economic conditions favorable to United States interests.

A graphic example * is provided by the American Institute for Research (Pittsburgh, Pennsylvania). The AIR prepared a report for the Defense Department's Advanced Research

---

* There are literally scores of these projects. We have selected this project in Thailand as representative. The reader is referred to two particularly good references in this field—*The University-Military-Police Complex, A Directory and Related Documents*, published by the North American Congress on Latin America (New York: 1970, 88pp.), and *African Studies in America; The Extended Family*, published by Africa Research Group (Cambridge, Mass., October 1969, 53pp.).

Projects Agency (ARPA) in December, 1967, entitled: "Counter-Insurgency in Thailand: The Impact of Economic, Social and Political Action Programs." It is well worth quoting from it at length because nothing else will convey the full nature of this research project.

The Report opens with a two-page description of the problem in Thailand:

> . . . The struggle between an established government and subversive or insurgent forces involves three different types of operations. The first is to make inputs into the social system that will gain the active support of an ever-increasing proportion of the local population. Threats, promises, ideological appeals and tangible benefits are the kinds of inputs that are most frequently used. The second is to reduce or interdict the flow of competing inputs being made by the opposing side by installing anti-infiltration devices, cutting communication lines, assassinating key spokesmen, strengthening retaliatory mechanisms, and similar preventive measures. The third is to counteract or neutralize the political successes already achieved by groups committed to the "wrong" side. This typically involves direct military confrontation.
>
> The social scientist can make significant contributions to the design of all three operations. But it is in the first area—that of designing programs to win or strengthen public support—that he is expected to take the lead; and it is with this area that we are chiefly concerned.[18]

The Report suggests that the social sciences have not as yet developed a satisfactory method for evaluating the real effectiveness of its various programs; but, the Report goes on:

> This proposal describes a program of research and development that will hopefully resolve this basic problem as it applies to the counter-insurgency effort in Thailand, and provide a basis for generalization to other programs in other cultures. Its specific objectives are to:
>
> 1) devise reliable and valid techniques for assessing the outcomes of counter-insurgency programs in Thailand;
>
> 2) apply these techniques to specified action programs to provide administrators and planners with operationally useful feed-

back data, indices of present status, and diagnosis pertinent to future program design;

3) assist the Royal Thai Government in expanding indigenous capabilities for the continuing application and refinement of assessment techniques;

4) provide ARPA with guide lines for extending the approach to other countries; and

5) provide to the social sciences an improved measurement methodology applicable to other problems and other settings *including the United States*.[19] [Emphasis added—B.A.]

The Report discusses in detail various technical and methodological problems. For example, researchers need to "interview" two types of informants in the country being "studied." First, villagers, with knowledge of the normal conditions, customs, and so forth, and second:

We shall also have to determine the behavioral objectives of the insurgents, specifying in detail what it is that the insurgents want, target communities, organizations and individuals. The second class of informants, therefore, should consist of samples of experienced insurgents. . . .

. . . it will be assumed that the degree to which a disposing condition has changed can be observed not only as a result of its impact on target behaviors at a time of insurgent pressure, but also through its impact on every-day kinds of behavior and everyday kinds of situations. Identifying the everyday behaviors that are indicators of target behavior will be the common goal toward which each of the different methodological approaches will be directed.[20]

The Report discusses the technical problems encountered in obtaining the desired behavorial patterns:

A weak stimulus, such as the instructions given to a village by an unknown government official, will probably become stronger after a sequence of positive personal interactions. A strong stimulus, such as the threat of physical violence as the penalty for non-compliance will probably become weaker after a sequence of experiences in which the individual finds that this threat is no longer carried out as it was in the past.

. . . The specific effect of most stimulus elements is not absolute, but rather dependent on certain other circumstances that obtain at the same time the response is to be made . . .

. . . The offer of food in exchange for certain services affords a convenient example. If this has in the past been a strong stimulus, it can probably be weakened by increasing local agricultural production. If it has been a weak or neutral stimulus, it can probably be strengthened by burning the crops . . .[21]

One of the most revealing (and terrifying) aspects of this prospectus is the technification of language, the "objectification" of people: ". . . informants should *consist of samples of experienced insurgents* . . ."; "Threats, promises, ideological appeals and tangible benefits are the kinds of *inputs* [one is speaking of an electrical system, perhaps] that are most frequently used . . .," etc.

The descent of anthropology and other disciplines into the unqualified, practical service of imperialism provoked a formidable struggle within the academic community. The opposition does not yet represent a majority of social scientists, but it does constitute a vocal, militant and growing minority. Disclosure of the intrigue in Thailand, for example, forced a confrontation in the American Anthropological Association in which the chairman of its Ethics Committee, Eric R. Wolf, wrote to the anthropologists whose names repeatedly appeared in the incriminating documents asking them for clarification, in that:

Since these documents contradict in spirit and in letter the resolutions of the American Anthropological Association concerning clandestine and secret research, we feel that they raise the most serious issues for the scientific integrity of our profession. We shall, therefore, call the attention of the Anthropological Association to these most serious matters.[21]

A storm of controversy ensued, and on May 2, 1970, The Ethics Committee formally concluded:

Our examination of the documents available to us pertaining to consultation, research and related activities in Thailand convinces us that anthropologists are being used in large programs of counter-insurgency whose effects should be of grave concern to the Association. These programs comprise efforts at the manipulation of people on a giant scale and intertwine straightforward anthropological research with overt and covert counter-insurgency activities in such a way as to threaten the future of anthropological research in South-East Asia and other parts of the world.[23]

Counter-insurgency is not designed solely for international consumption. On the contrary, increasing emphasis is given to developing techniques for the containment of domestic insurgency as the general social crisis in the United States grows deeper and more profound. This AIR prospectus for example emphasizes its domestic relevance:

The potential applicability of the findings in the United States will also receive special attention. In many ways our key domestic programs, *especially those directed at disadvantaged sub-cultures,* are highly similar to those discernible in this proposal; and the application of the Thai findings at home constitute a potentially most significant project contribution . . .[14] [Emphasis added.—B.A.]

The behavioral and social scientists, in fact, play a prominent role in devising techniques for the containment of actually or potentially disruptive social forces within the country. In January, 1971, the Ford Foundation announced that it was providing support for programs and research related to problems of American's white working-class population. "The grants," the Foundation said, "are intended to widen understanding of the continuing role of ethnicity in American life and to explore the economic and social roots of working-class American anxiety and to explore ways of mitigating their discontent." [25]

The concentration of behavioralists in containing widespread social disaffection is reflective of the assumption—essential for the maintenance of the status quo—that the protest and

PENTAGON SPONSORED FOREIGN POLICY RESEARCH

According to information provided by the Department of Defense, the Pentagon spent a total of $45.4 million on social and behavioral science research in fiscal year 1969. $48.6 million was budgeted for these purposes in FY 1970; of this amount, $5.2 million is for studies with foreign policy implications and $7.5 million is for foreign area research. Reprinted below is a partial listing of current Pentagon-sponsored social research projects with foreign policy implications. Source: * *Congressional Record*, May 1, 1969, pp. S4418–23.

Abbreviations:

ARPA: Advanced Research Projects Agency
CRESS: Center for Research in Social Systems
DoD: Department of Defense
IDA: Institute for Defense Analysis
OASD/ISA: Office of the Asst. Secy. of Defense for International Security Affairs
RAC: Research Analysis Corp.
SDC: System Development Corp.
SRI: Stanford Research Institute
Policy Planning Studies with Foreign Policy Implications
SPONSOR: DEPARTMENT OF THE ARMY, OCRD
(Note: Information concerning 21 projects is classified and, therefore, not included in this listing)

Project Title	Project Description	Contractor/Investigator
Beliefs and habits of certain foreign populations significance for psychological operations (U).	Classified	CRESS ....

* North American Congress on Latin America, the university-military-policy complex, a directory and related documents, New York, 1970, pp. 58–62.

Project Title	Project Description	Contractor/Investigator
U.S. Army psychological operations requirements worldwide.	Overview, ordering, integration of PSYOPS knowledge and thinking to provide guidance for planning, operations, training, research.	CRESS
Development of critical target analysis information for the U.S. strategic psychological operations in Southeast Asia.	Identification of questions to be used as essential elements of information to collect information required in conduct of PSYOPS.	CRESS
Combating insurgent infrastructure in Southeast Asia.	Research on techniques to eliminate Communist insurgent movement in South Vietnam. Application of findings to dissimilar environment of second country in SEA.	CRESS
Social processes relevant to military planning for stability studies of African groups.	Study of African socio-political structures, dynamics, and leadership resources and attitudes.	CRESS
Research on civic action and community assistance programs in Panama.	Identification of techniques and procedures that contribute to operational effectiveness of military civic action programs.	CRESS
Guidelines for effective management of foreign national employees of the U.S. Army.	Survey of experiences of U.S. supervisory personnel and development of data bank of critical incidents and cultural differences relevant to civilian personnel operations.	Human Resources Research Office

Project Title	Project Description	Contractor/Investigator
SPONSOR: U.S. ARMY MEDICAL RESEARCH AND DEVELOPMENT COMMAND		
Comprehensive epidemiologic studies in developing countries.	Study of disease conditions and vectors in selected rural populations.	The Johns Hopkins Univ., Alfred Buck, M.D.
The culture of health and illness in a Southeast Asian village.	Beliefs and behavior relation to health and illness in a village in Thailand.	University of Penn., Gertrude Marlowe.
Interpersonal perception and the psychological adjustment of group members.	Study of group effectiveness in divergent cultural groups.	University of Illinois, Fred E. Fiedler.
SPONSOR: NAVY, OFFICE OF NAVAL RESEARCH		
Anthropological research to assist Navy strategic planning.	Investigator will combine anthropological variables with econometric techniques in order to conceptualize and predict mobility in foreign military hierarchies. Will be completed in May (1969)	University of Texas, I. Buchler
Identification of factors influencing the effectiveness of management and leadership.	Field data collection on the training, leadership characteristics, preferences, and effectiveness of foreign managerial personnel and trainees.	University of Rochester, B. M. Bass.
SPONSOR: AIR FORCE OFFICE OF SCIENTIFIC RESEARCH (OAR)		
Information system for analysis of a closed society.	Method for coding and analyzing data on a strategic area (Chicom)	University of Calif., Berkeley, Dr. C. Y. Glock.

Project Title	Project Description	Contractor/Investigator
SPONSOR: AIR FORCE OFFICE OF SCIENTIFIC RESEARCH (OAR)—Continued		
Perception of threat, evaluation of stress and decision-making.	Study of the way individuals and groups including civilian populations, their leaders and military organizations are likely to respond to the threats inherent in aerospace warfare and other impending dangers.	Catholic University, Washington, D.C., A. Frances.
Studies in the processes of political development and revolutionary behavior.	Strategic analysis of selected developing countries from documentary and other available data.	University of Penn., Foreign Policy Research Inst., Kintner & Schwartz.
SPONSOR: ARPA/BEHAVIORAL SCIENCES—DEFENSE RESEARCH DONE IN FOREIGN AREAS		
Cross-national studies of conflict dynamics and resolution.	Present understanding of bargaining and negotiating behavior comes from research done solely with American subjects. This project cross-checks such knowledge by using similar data from European subjects to provide American military personnel with ability to deal effectively with European counterparts. Overseas work done entirely by foreign nationals in a cooperative program. Expires August 1970.	UCLA, Dr. Harold Kelley

Project Title	Project Description	Contractor/Investigator
SPONSOR: ARPA/BEHAVIORAL SCIENCES—DEFENSE RESEARCH DONE IN UNITED STATES BUT RELATED TO FOREIGN AREAS		
Military implications of international bargaining and negotiations.	Build predictive theories of bargaining and negotiating processes to avoid, limit and resolve military conflict. Increase understanding of the relation of such processes to international politico-military systems through development and use of computer simulations. Intermediate results in use by joint War Games Agency and Industrial College of the Armed Forces.	SDC, Dr. Gerald Shure, Northwestern Univ., Dr. Harold Guetzkow.
Strategic analysis of social conflict.	Continuation of Dr. Schelling's work to improve understanding of revolutionary processes.	Harvard University, Dr. Thomas Schelling.
Prediction of international military capabilities and events.	To develop quantitative methodology and theory for use of publicly available data (U.N. news media, etc.) to improve predictions and understanding of actions by foreign nations.	University of Hawaii, Dr. R. Rummel.

Project Title	Project Description	Contractor/Investigator
SPONSOR: ARMY, OFFICE, DEPUTY CHIEF OF STAFF, MILITARY OPERATIONS (ODSCOPS)		
Note: Information concerning 20 projects, including all projects sponsored by ARPA/AGILE, are classified and not included in this listing.		
Strategic analysis of subsaharan Africa, 1969 (SASSA) (8 substudies).	Includes studies of U.S. strategic interests, environmental trends, and U.S. policies and programs.	RAC ....
Strategic analysis of Europe, 1969 (SAEUR) (6 substudies).	Includes studies of French foreign policy, European trade prospects, development of Siberia and Soviet-Japanese trade.	RAC ....
Strategic Analysis of Southeast Asia, 1969 (SASEA) (8 substudies).	Includes analysis of Malaysian foreign policy, regional military co-operation, and Australian foreign and military policy.	RAC ....
Latin American nuclear free zone (LANFZ).	Will address questions concerning U.S. bases, installations, and activities in the zone of application of LANFZ Army plans for the defense of the Panama Canal.	RAC ....

Project Title	Project Description	Contractor/Investigator
SPONSOR: AIR FORCE, OFFICE, DEPUTY CHIEF OF STAFF, RESEARCH AND DEVELOPMENT		
Chinese military and foreign policy	A continuing analysis of the background and fundamental characteristics of Chinese foreign and military policies to elucidate their implications for U.S. policy. Research provides background for consultations with Air Staff officials and for inputs to inter-departmental studies, such as work on strategic posture toward China.	Rand, A. Hsieh
European security issues	A continuing examination of trends in the political and military relations of European States, including possible changes in European security arrangements, and national developments affecting the overall European military posture.	Rand, F. C. Ikle
Soviet military and foreign policy	A continuing study of Soviet military doctrine, use of military strength for political purposes, foreign policy, and political institutions in the Soviet Union and East European States.	Rand, A. Horelick

Project Title	Project Description	Contractor/Investigator
SPONSOR: AIR FORCE, OFFICE, DEPUTY CHIEF OF STAFF, RESEARCH AND DEVELOPMENT—Continued		
Sino-Soviet economic potential	A continuing study of the economic background of Soviet and Communist Chinese military power. Presently it includes studies of outlays, employment, and organizational problems in Soviet R.&D., Soviet foreign economic relations, and Chinese civil aviation.	Rand, C. Hoeffding
The role of the military in Indonesia	An analysis in support of Air Force plans and intelligence of the role of the military in the developing political, economic, and defense structure of Indonesia, and the probable role of Indonesia in the larger context of U.S. security interests in SEA.	Rand, G. J. Pauker
SPONSOR: OASD/ISA		
Development of a planning, programming and budgeting system (PPBS) for U.S. foreign economic decisions.	Development of an analytical framework or model which can be used to identify how resources are organized and focused in achieving U.S. foreign policy objectives.	Planning Research Corporation ....

Project Title	Project Description	Contractor/Investigator
SPONSOR: OASD/ISA—Continued		
Insurgent forces	Development and analysis of certain U.S. experiences in Vietnam, aiming at generalization applicable to future U.S. policymaking.	Rand
Eastern Europe	A series of studies on political, economic, and military trends in Europe, including security arrangements.	IDA
Communist China	A broad effort to correlate and evaluate data on Communist China's political, economic, and military objectives and to determine the foreign policy implications for the United States.	IDA
An analytical summary of U.S. security for educational and research purposes.	An examination of various U.S. national security issues and their relationships.	Hudson Institute

disaffection is primarily a reflection of individual and psychological infirmity rather than social decay. Such psychological
explanations, as Howard Zinn suggested, emphasize the irrationality of the protester rather than the irrationality of that
which produces protest. He continued:

> It seems much easier for us to believe that the Abolitionists
> were vehement because they were up-ward striving than that they
> grasped in some small way the horror of slavery. It is easier to
> believe that students have "intense, unresolved Oedipal feelings,
> a tremendous attachment to their mothers, and a violent hostility
> to their fathers" [quoting from Lewis Feuer's analysis of the
> student movement] rather than that they are outraged at a society
> which (speaking precisely) will not let them live.[26]

The resolution of conflict is then seen in psychological
rather than social terms. It is an individual rather than a
collective problem. That is, the theory insures that the socio-
political institutions and the economic relationships they
maintain will remain intact. An analysis of the social functions
of the prison system in the United States * offers a penetrating
view of behavioralist theory and its practical implications.

NATIONAL INSTITUTE OF LAW ENFORCEMENT
AND CRIMINAL JUSTICE
1969 RESEARCH CONTRACTS (PARTIAL LISTING)
Source: ** First Annual Report 1969 Law Enforcement Assistance
Administration

NI-032 $25,000   From 6/15/69 to 12/15/69
Grantee: University of California at Berkeley
Title: Physical Evidence Utilization
Abstract: Examine and evaluate impact on crime control of vari-
ous criminalistics operations.

* What follows is a revised version of an article by the present writer
on the "Social Functions of the Prisons in the United States" which
appears in the book co-authored by herself and Angela Y. Davis, *If
They Come In the Morning,* The Third Press, New York, 1971.
** As compiled by the North American Congress on Latin America,
The University-Military-Police Complex, A Directory and Related
Documents, N.Y. 1970, pp. 73–79.

NI-041 $21,955 From 7/1/69 to 12/31/69
Grantee: University of California at Santa Barbara
Title: Econometric Study of Economy-Related Crimes
Abstract: This is a study to determine the interrelationships among economic, age, education, and law enforcement factors for a selected age group of offenders committing economic crimes on the arrest rates for these crimes. This is an attempt to view this kind of criminal activity in a broad enough context to determine not only where and at what levels crime may be expected, but also to identify the critical factors leading to economic crimes.

NI-026 $50,141 From 6/30/69 to 9/30/70
Grantee: Carnegie-Mellon University, Pittsburgh, Pennsylvania
Title: Analysis of a Statewide Criminal Justice System
Abstract: A study of the entire criminal justice system at the State Level (Pennsylvania) is being done so that a clear understanding of the interrelationships among the elements of a State criminal justice system can be developed from a broad vantage point, and thereby detect and hopefully avoid bottlenecks and conflicts which occur within the elements of any system which must function together smoothly. The results of this study will be applicable with appropriate modifications to many other States and will furnish an important planning tool for allocating resources to obtain an effective state criminal justice system.

NI-023 $49,663 From 6/30/69 to 1/31/70
Grantee: George Washington University, Washington, D.C.
Title: Development and Implementation of a Behavioral/Systems Approach to Prevention and Control of Delinquency and Crime.
Abstract: This study will analyze the effectiveness of our social institutions, education, welfare courts and corrections in the control and treatment of delinquents. It is expected to provide an explanatory framework for social behavior and a program for the management of the general system.

NI-039 $101,083 From 6/30/69 to 5/31/70
Grantee: Georgetown University Law School, Washington, D.C.
Title: Training Policemen to Deal with Family Disturbances
Abstract: The purpose of the proposal is to train police to deal

with "family disturbances" in addition to law enforcement duties, the apprehension of criminals and crime prevention training. Specifically they will be trained to deal with: (1) offenses against family and children, (2) incorrigible juveniles, (3) family disturbances, and (4) "disturbing the peace" calls.

NI-047 $118,800   From 7/1/69 to 6/30/70
Grantee: Institute for Behavioral Research, Silver Spring, Maryland
Title: Develop a Study of Alternatives to Punishment in Maintaining Law and Order
Abstract: This research project has two objectives: The first objective is to study alternatives to punitive law enforcement measures, such as fines and incarcerations, by investigating the feasibility of preventive systems based on constructive re-enforcement. The second objective is to evaluate a study completed by the Institute for Behavioral Research at the National Training School for Boys. This study used the technique of operant conditioning to change the behavior of 41 selected inmates.

NI-031 $101,914   From 9/1/68 to 7/31/69
Grantee: Institute for the Study of Crime & Delinquency, Sacramento, California
Title: Model Community Corrections Program—Phase II
Abstract: This continuation grant will provide second stage funds to construct a model community correctional program designed to interface with a typical county criminal justice system in providing disposition alternatives for client control and treatment through community based programs evolved from planning activities conducted under a previous LEA Act grant.

NI-027 $50,714   From 6/30/69 to 6/30/70
Grantee: University of Michigan, Ann Arbor
Title: Methodological Studies of Crime Classification
Abstract: The accurate assessment of the volume of crime and of particular kinds of crime is the objective of this study. It is expected to evaluate the factors that affect the classification of major index crimes and to develop ways of estimating base population for victim statistics.

NI-040 $59,130   From 7/1/69 to 6/30/70
Grantee: Institute for Social Research, The Regents of the University of Michigan, Ann Arbor.
Title: Alternative Responses to School Crisis
Abstract: It is a goal of this project to work with three schools to try out several models of alternative and more creative response to crisis and disruption. It is also a goal of this project to develop and demonstrate programs to create new links between protesting student groups, educational leaders and police officials. Representatives of law enforcement systems need to understand better the particular issues and potentials in student-school crises, and the ways they may be most helpful to students and educators. The latter groups need a better understanding of the potential role of law enforcement systems, and the implications of school unrest for local police and judiciary agencies.

NI-044 $100,000   From 6/30/69 to 6/30/70
Grantee: Midwest Research Institute, Kansas City, Missouri
Title: A Systems Analysis of Criminalistics Operations
Abstract: This study will be a comprehensive systems analysis of the crime laboratory in law enforcement and criminal justice. Emphasis will be placed on quantifying the knowledge of present experts in criminalistics so as to allow a structured approach to both enhance and multiply this expertise to the benefit of all areas of the country. The primary goal of the study is to recommend systems of criminalistics operations that would meet cost/benefit criteria while serving the needs of local communities, regional areas and the nation.

NI-030 $35,714.20   From 6/30/69 to 6/30/71
Grantee: University of Pennsylvania, Philadelphia
Title: Patrolmen in Urban Environments
Abstract: This project is designed to study the technical and cultural processes by which a citizen is enrolled, trained, and acculturated into an urban police force. Observation will be carried out in a program of systematic field work extending over a full year and will cover the range of ecological types in American cities. Police contacts in international situations will be given particular attention.

NI-009 $102,148   From 6/30/69 to 6/30/70
Grantee: Wayne State University, Detroit, Michigan
Title: Study of the Police Vehicle
Abstract: The overall goal of this project is to understand the role of the vehicle in relation to police departments and from this understanding will come a better vehicle for police use, a better set of policies for its use, and a better program for procurement, replacement and operation. The objective in the broad sense is to aid in achieving better police operations within the best cost framework.

Officially it is maintained that there are no prisons in the United States. There are Departments of Corrections, and there are "correctional facilities" equipped with "educational programs," "vocational training" and the necessary "psychiatric therapy." There are also no prisoners in the United States; there are only "inmates." There are most certainly no *political* prisoners in the United States; only "terrorists" and those who "perpetrate criminal violence."

The semantic somersaults of the behavioralist-prison bureaucracy serve a calculated and specific ideological function. Once we penetrate this linguistic shield we have the key to understanding the social and political functions of the prison system.

The criminologists affirm the dominant theoretical assumptions of the social and behavioral scientists in general that the social order is functionally stable and fundamentally just. This basic premise means that the theory *must* then assume the moral depravity of the prisoner. There can be no other logical explanation for his incarceration. As George Jackson put it: "The textbooks on criminology like to advance the idea that the prisoners are mentally defective. There is only the merest suggestion that the system itself is at fault . . ."[27] Indeed, the assistant warden at San Quentin, who is by profession a clinical psychologist, tells us that prisoners suffer from "retarded emotional growth." The warden continues: "The first goal of the prison is to isolate the people the community doesn't want at large. Safe confinement is the goal. The second obligation is a reasonably good housekeeping job, the old humanitarian treatment concept." [28] That is, once the prisoner is adequately confined and isolated, he may be treated for his emotional and psychological maladies—which he is assumed to suffer by virtue of the fact that he is a prisoner. We have a completely circular method of reasoning. It is a closed-circuit system from which there is no apparent escape.

The alleged criminal characteristics of the prisoner must, in accord with this logical sequence, arise from *within* the prisoner himself. According to the behavioralist, the criminal has acquired certain *psychological* characteristics which dictate his pattern of criminal behavior. To "unacquire" these characteristics a leading behavioral scientist, James V. McConnell, explains that: "We have but two means of educating people or rats or flatworms—we can either reward them or punish them . . ." [29] The treatment for what McConnell calls "brainwashing the criminals" to ultimately restructure their entire personality is an alternating sequence of reward and punishment (including especially so-called shock treatment) until the prisoner has "learned" what the society defines as non-criminal behavior.

The source of criminality then is psychological rather than social. The solution to the problem is obvious: quarantine the afflicted individuals; then subject them to treatment. Hence we have *correctional* facilities rather than prisons; and we have *inmates* (as in an asylum for the insane) rather than prisoners.

As Marcuse has so aptly described it: "The language of the prevailing Law and Order, validated by the courts and by the police, is not only the voice but also the deed of suppression. This language not only defines and condemns the Enemy, it also *creates* him; and this creation is not the Enemy as he really is but rather as he must be in order to perform his function for the Establishment . . ." [30]

In this instance the Enemy is the criminal or the prisoner. The behavioralist view of the criminal *has almost nothing to do with breaking the law*. Professor Theodore Sarbin of the University of California criminology department put it this way: ". . . membership in the class of people known as 'law-breakers' *is not* distributed according to economic or social status, but membership in the class 'criminals' *is* distributed according to social or economic status . . ." [31]

Example: The ten executives of the General Electric Company convicted in 1961 of price-fixing involving tens of millions of dollars are law-breakers, and some of them actually served some months in prison. Nevertheless, the society does not consider them criminals.

By way of contrast, a Chicano or Black youth alleged to have stolen $10.00 from a grocery store is not only considered a criminal by the society, but this assumption allows the police to act with impunity. They can shoot him, and chances are it will be ruled justifiable homicide in a coroner's inquest.

What then is the political function of the criminal and the prisoner as they are created and described by the bourgeois penologists and criminologists?

Consider penology as one aspect of the theory and practice of containment on the domestic front; that is, consider penology as the confinement and treatment of people who are actually or potentially disruptive of the social system.

In an increasing number of ways the entire judicial and penal system involving the police, the courts, the prisons and the parole boards has become a mechanism through which the ruling powers seek to maintain their physical and psychological control, or the threat of control, over millions of working people, especially young people, and most especially Black and Brown young people.

Consider the operations of the California Adult Authority. Roughly 97 percent of the male prisoners in that state are eventually released from prison—all of them via parole. A man is sentenced to a term in prison—very often an indeterminate sentence such as from one year to life. In addition to whatever time he actually serves in prison, he is released on parole for five, even ten or more years. The conditions of his parole are appalling. For example, he can be stopped and searched at any time; his house can be entered without a warrant; he needs the permission of his parole officer to borrow money, to marry, to drive a car, to change his job, to leave the county, and so forth. If parole is revoked the prisoner is returned to custody without trial to complete his full sentence. Members of the Adult Authority are appointed by the Governor. They are answerable to no one.

This entire complex is a system of tyranny under which an ever-increasing number of working people—especially again Black and Brown people—are forced to live.

As such it is a prelude to fascism. Indeed, Professor Herbert Packer of the Stanford Law School is exactly right in his conclusion that ". . . the inevitable end of the behavioral view is preventive detention . . ." [32]

For once you accept the behavioralist view of the criminal as morally depraved or mentally defective it is perfectly logical to preventively detain *all* persons who manifest such tendencies and are therefore *potential* criminals. Thus, in April, 1970, a leading physician and close associate of President Nixon proposed that the Government begin the mass testing of 6- to 8-year-old children to determine if they have criminal-behavior tendencies. He then suggested "treatment camps" for the severely disturbed child and the young hard-core criminal.

Even more consequential in terms of their potential political impact are the proposals of Edward C. Banfield, a professor of Urban Government at Harvard, and the chairman of President Nixon's task force on the Model Cities Program. Banfield's analysis of the urban crisis exactly coincides with the behavioralists' view of the criminal. That is, the cause of the urban crisis lies in the existence of what Banfield calls the "lower classes" who are poverty-prone. These lower classes are of course working people, and Black and Brown people in particular. They are, Banfield would have us believe, morally depraved and mentally defective. For example, Banfield describes people of the lower classes as:

feeble . . . suspicious and hostile, aggressive yet dependent . . . no attachment to community, neighbors or friends . . . lives in the slum and sees little or no reason to complain . . . does not care how dirty and dilapidated his housing is . . . nor does he mind the inadequacy of such public facilities as schools, parks and libraries . . . features that make the slum repellent to others actually please him . . . prefers near-destitution without work to abundance with it . . . the morality of lower-class culture is pre-conventional, which means that the individual's actions are influenced not by conscience but only by a sense of what he can get away with . . .[33]

Banfield's description of the lower class is in fact a description of the criminal. And it is precisely at this moment when the description of the lower class and the description of the criminal *coincide* that we have a central aspect of the ideological basis for fascism and genocide. This is exactly Banfield's program.

Summarizing the most salient points in the Professor's program we find these proposals: that the government try to reduce unemployment by eliminating all minimum-wage laws and by repealing all laws which give trade unions "mono-polistic powers," e.g., the closed shop; that the government abolish all child labor laws and cut compulsory education from 12 to 9 years; that it change poverty definitions from those which encompass relative standards of living to a "fixed standard" and that it encourage or require all persons who fall into this fixed poverty standard to live in an institution or semi-institution; that the government institute vigorous birth control measures for the incompetent poor and send their children to public nurseries; that the government intensify police control and specifically permit the police to "stop and frisk" and to make misdemeanor arrests on probable cause; and that the government "abridge to an appropriate degree the freedom of those who in the opinion of a court are ex-tremely likely to commit violent crimes . . ." [34]

This is a *fascist* program. It is a *genocidal* program. It is, in the final analysis, the ultimate logic of the behavioralist view. Behaviorism represents, *epitomizes,* the degeneration and disintegration of liberalism philosophically, theoretically and functionally.

New techniques of communication and the monopoliza-tion of the mass media provide behavioral and social scientists with hitherto unknown means for extraordinarily subtle and intricate forms of manipulation and control. Likewise the propagation of false consciousness assumes hitherto unknown dimensions. It becomes an increasingly important means through which the corporate state seeks to contain and divert all opposing social forces.

Linguistic form, for example (that is, the use of key words in a particular sequence) becomes a substitute for substance. The final absurdity in this charade was the nationally tele-vised State of the Union message by President Nixon in January, 1971, in which he called for a "New American Revolution." The idiotic quintessence of this performance was brilliantly captured by Jules Feiffer in a cartoon strip, in which the President assumes the physical appearance of a bearded militant, shouting revolutionary slogans, and then ends his performance with a modest "Thank you," informing the audience, "In next month's speech on foreign policy I will do my impression of Gandhi."

Words and phrases are manipulated and twisted to fit the contours of imperialist intrigue. For example, the President makes a major foreign policy speech on Southeast Asia. Marcuse exposes its inner logic: ". . . We work for peace; antithesis: we prepare for war (or even: we wage war); unification of opposites: preparing for war *is* working for peace. Peace is redefined as necessarily, in the prevailing situation, including preparation for war (or even war) . . ." [35]

Similarly, a presidential advisor makes a major policy statement on a domestic crisis. We believe in and work for racial equality. However, we must equivocate in the enforcement of the Constitution, and in the extirpation of racism, because to do either or both induces further manifestations of racism. Racism, then, is a product of the psychological and personal feelings held by many otherwise well-meaning and decent individuals. We need to assume a posture of "benign neglect" to allow moderation and reason to prevail. Thus, the source of racism is racism; and the neglect of crisis yields moderation, therefore reason, therefore solution.

There is a constant elevation and expansion of the ideological struggle within the imperialist country, which requires greater degrees of intellectual sophistication to unravel. It is a decisive arena of revolutionary struggle for the consciousness of oppression, and the comprehension of its source are the prerequisites of any and all forms of effective resistance.

Our point is not to propose that all social and behavioral

scientists are evil; nor to suggest that all social and behavioral science as such is oppressive. Rather, the point is that regardless of the motivation of the scholar, his work can and often does become a weapon of imperialist oppression. The university can no longer engage in the abstract pursuit of scholarship. The level of science and technology, and the interrelationship between technology and social change, is such that none of the sciences can be extracted from a social context. There is no longer anything so abstract, subtle, remote or theoretically pure that it cannot be applied to imperialist intrigue, demogoguery or violence. The university is *already committed* to social purposes. The point is not to debate the merits of this commitment. The question is: what social purposes are to be advanced, and for whose benefit?

The tension and conflict in the university is not derived from its practical commitment to social change *per se*. Rather it derives from the prevailing commitment of the social sciences to imperialist intrigue. This flies in the face of the humanist and radical dynamic of learning itself. The tension between the intrinsic qualities of learning on the one hand, and the exploitative and oppressive essence of society on the other, has always existed to some degree. The most obvious example is the long and brutal conflict between ecclesiastical doctrine and scientific truth (which, of course, also presented itself as a formidable socio-economic struggle against the power of the Church). Today this historic tension between the qualities of learning and those of society, has acquired a new intensity, precisely because the university is now a practical instrument for social change.

This fact was demonstrated in its most elementary form at the 1966 national meeting of the American Anthropological Association which passed a resolution that condemned "the use of napalm, chemical defoliants, harmful gases, bombing, the torture and killing of political prisoners and prisoners of war, and the international and deliberate policies of genocide or forced transportation of populations." It asked "all governments" to put an end to their use and at once "proceed as rapidly as possible to a peaceful settlement of the war in Vietnam." When this Vietnam resolution was first introduced the chairman judged it to be "political" and ruled it out of order since the Association's stated purpose, he said, is to advance the science of anthropology and to further the professional interests of American anthropologists. The resolution was saved when one member jumped up and exclaimed: "Genocide is not in the professional interests of anthropologists! " [36]

This process of politicalization is irreversible. As the social sciences are used for the practical consolidation of the system, the protest of the intellectual can no longer be expressed in purely theoretical terms. Aloofness from politics is self-deception. Neutrality is a myth. Passivity *is* compliance. The dissenting intellectual must move from protest to resistance. For only by breaking out of the operational mold altogether, only by totally rejecting the operational limitations on conceptual thought, can the behavioral or social scientist abandon his servitude. In this sense there is no ideological "center" in which the intellectual may vacillate; only a *radical* theoretical departure from the operational view provides him with an authentic alternative. Since the university is already inexorably social and political, this radical theoretical departure necessarily gives rise to practical forms of political opposition.

Further, scholarly and scientific work has become more and more of a *collective* enterprise—a reflection of the increasingly social character of production.[37] While intellectuals have traditionally tended toward individual forms of protest reflecting the former atomization of their work (this individualistic tendency is still very pronounced) the new socialized conditions of their work now makes possible *collective* (*organized*) opposition.

The intelligentsia as a whole is forced into the arena of practical politics; and an intense political struggle unfolds within the university—a theoretical and practical struggle—between those who service the ideological and practical needs of imperialism, and those who resist such service.

5 THE STATE AND THE UNIVERSITY

As the university emerges as a constituent part of the productive process—a center for scientific research and development (R & D), for the practical consolidation of the social system, and for scientific, technical and professional training—the state must vastly increase its financial support of higher education, and it undertakes its direction and control. One scholar aptly described the relationship: "Of all the inter-penetrations that between multiversity and federal government is most significant. So completely have the two come to rely upon one another that the relationship might . . . be considered a symbiosis . . ."[1] The state is the mechanism through which the academy becomes an *integral* part of the productive process.

In his polemic on *The State,* Lenin wrote:

> . . . the state is an organ of class *domination,* an organ of *oppression* of one class by another; its aim is the creation of "order" which legalises and perpetuates this oppression by moderating the collisions between the classes . . .[2]

Marx suggested another (secondary) dimension in the role of the state:

. . . supervision and management is naturally required wherever
. the direct process of production assumes the form of combined
social process, and not of the isolated labourers of independent
producers . . .[3]

From the Marxist view then, the state assumes two distinct
but closely related functions, one derived of class domination
and exploitation, the other from the social character of the
productive process which requires supervision and regulation. The coercive and oppressive functions of the imperialist
state are primary and decisive. Therefore, all of the anti-
human priorities and values of the imperialist state are foisted
upon the university to an unprecedented degree in the present period. This is the source of still another aspect of the
crisis in the university. Furthermore, then, the revolutionary
transformation of society and the break-up of the bourgeois
state apparatus will effect the university as no previous revolution has.

The continuing socialization of the production process—
that is, the expansion, integration, and interdependence of
the industrial, social, and natural processes—is accelerated
by the scientific and technological revolution. Intensified socialization, in turn, causes the initial capital investment and
future capital expenditures for industrial development to rise
precipitously. For example in 1941 the federal government
and private industry combined spent only $880 million for
research and development. In 1964 the total annual sum was
over $18 billion. It is easy to see that at a certain point the
capital necessary for industrial expansion and development
exceeds the financial resources of private industry and banking (individually and even combined). (This difficulty in
financing research and development is aggravated by the
tendency toward a declining *rate* of profit under capitalist
relations of production as modern machinery is introduced.)
It becomes necessary for the state to intervene to provide

Expenditures for Research and Development in the U.S.: 1940-1969.

millions of dollars

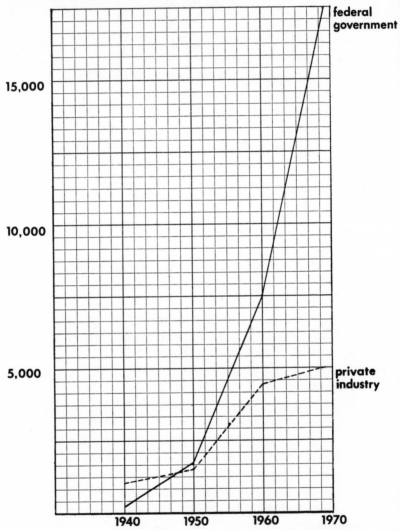

Compiled from data from the National Science Foundation and the U.S. Department of Commerce.

monetary aid to private corporations in the form of capital and/or land. Engels predicted that the state would ultimately have to undertake the direction of production. He suggested that this conversion into state property would be felt first in the great institutions for intercourse and communication—the post-offices, the telegraphs and the railways.[4]

The intervention of the state cannot be arrested, for to accomplish that the industrial process itself would have to be stopped and reversed. There is then a growing tendency toward a fusion between the state and finance capital—a fusion which is correlated to the level of scientific and' technical capability, i.e., the degree of socialization.

The fusion of the state with finance capital—that is, the emergence of state monopoly capital—does not represent a new (post-imperialist) stage in the development of capitalism. On the contrary, its earliest appearance is derived from the internal contradictions of capitalist relations of production (exploitative and overproductive). It is a product of the general crisis of capitalism. The intensification of this fusion between the state and finance capital, so evident today, is now, however, primarily determined by the requisite needs of the scientific-technological revolution (concentration of capital and social prognosis).[5] The fusion is intrinsic and vital to the system's social development. It represents the imperialist stage of capitalism in the era of its general crisis and in the era of the scientific and technological revolution.

The state necessarily assumes qualitatively new dimensions of power. It not only subsidizes, regulates, and coordinates the industrial process; but more and more it must organize, direct, and control it.

In the era of the scientific and technological revolution, with science emerging as a direct productive force, as the prerequisite of and motive force for technological progress, the initial capital investment and future (but projected) ex-

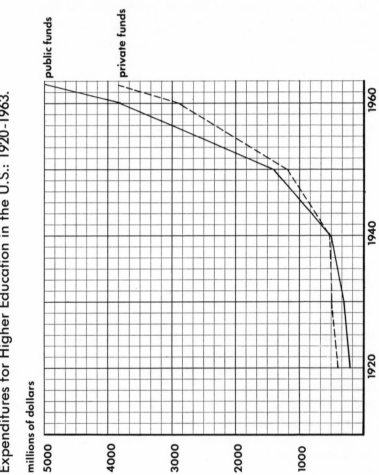

Expenditures for Higher Education in the U.S.: 1920-1963.

millions of dollars

public funds

private funds

Source: Role of the Federal Government in Education, Sidney W. Tiedt, New York: 1966, p.7.

penditures become so enormous (involving as they do not only production costs, but research and development), that the *sale of the commodity* (machinery or equipment) cannot be left to chance. On the contrary, a market must be guaranteed or production is not economically tenable. The state must subsidize research, development, and production, and it must seek to direct and control the market. In this way, the state, in the era of science, is not only the source of financial subsidy; it becomes the instrument of social planning.

As a result the social and behavioral sciences, as instruments for the practical consolidation of the system, assume a new dimension. That is, to guarantee the sale of commodities, the manipulation of consumer patterns becomes an *essential* aspect of the capitalist production process itself. For as Engels observed:

> No one knows how much of his particular article is coming on the market, nor how much of it will be wanted. No one knows whether his individual product will meet an actual demand, whether he will be able to make good his cost of production or even to sell his commodity at all. Anarchy reigns in socialized production.[6]

Modern techniques of market research, computer predictions, and so forth are used. These methods may bring occasional and momentary relief; but the tendencies described by Engels remain as long as capitalist relations of production—i.e., the private appropriation of socially produced wealth—are maintained. The deliberate creation of false needs, the promotion of a commodity fetishism, becomes as essential to the production process as the accessibility of raw materials.

Available data confirms this view of the new relationship between the university and the state. The total annual expenditures for higher education have increased at an astonishing rate in the past forty years; and since the early fifties that rate of increase has accelerated. In 1930 annual expenditures for higher education totalled $632 million; in 1950 it was $2½ billion; and in 1968 it was $17.2 billion. Clark Kerr, former president of the University of California, in a 1969 report prepared for the Carnegie Corporation predicted that by 1976 the total annual expenditures for higher education would exceed $40 billion.

As a consequence of the increased costs for research and development the federal government since 1950 has provided a growing proportion of the total funds for both. In 1940, private industry provided most of the money for R & D, and the federal government allotted less than half a billion dollars for it. In 1967 the situation was reversed. The federal government spent nearly $18 billion on R & D, while private industry spent less than $6 billion.

Correspondingly, federal expenditures to universities and colleges have jumped from $1.4 billion in 1963 to $3.3 billion in 1967. Clark Kerr, in the same report, recommended that in 1976 the federal government supply $10.5 billion to the colleges and universities. Of some 2,200 colleges and universities in the country, only 100 receive more than 85 percent of all federal funds to higher education.

Better than two-thirds of all federal funds to the universities are designated for research and development in the academic sciences.

Basic research is concentrated in the universities to a greater extent in the present period than ever before. Consequently, two-thirds of the federal funds to the universities come from the Department of Health, Education and Welfare (HEW); while less than 8 percent of these funds come from the Department of Defense (DOD). The National Aeronautics and Space Administration (NASA) supplies the universities with 3.7 percent of the federal funds; and the Atomic Energy Commission (AEC) supplies 3.3 percent of the total.

The reason for this funding arrangement—and the gap

between federal funds supplied by HEW as compared to those from DOD—is that the Defense Department and private industry are largely (though by no means entirely) responsible for development; while research is centered in the universities. The DOD for example was responsible for 58 percent of all federal obligations for development in 1968 (NASA, 29 percent; and AEC, 9 percent) while HEW was responsible for only 1 percent. Conversely, the largest sums of money for basic research from federal agencies in 1967 came from NASA, HEW, and the AEC, respectively. This is the reason that the bulk of the federal money to the universities is supplied by the Department of Health, Education and Welfare. Additionally, both NASA and the AEC have important research facilities administered by leading universities.

FEDERALLY FUNDED RESEARCH AND DEVELOPMENT
CENTERS ADMINISTERED BY UNIVERSITIES AND
COLLEGES
(as of June 1, 1968)
Department of Defense
  Department of the Army
    Army Mathematics Research Center (University of
      Wisconsin)
    Center for Research in Social Systems (American University)
    Human Resources Research Office (George Washington
      University)
  Department of the Navy
    Applied Physics Laboratory (Johns Hopkins University)
    Applied Physics Laboratory (University of Washington)
    Center for Naval Analyses (University of Rochester)
    Hudson Laboratories (Columbia University)
    Ordnance Research Laboratory (Pennsylvania State
      University)
  Department of the Air Force
    Lincoln Laboratory (Massachusetts Institute of Technology)
Department of Health, Education and Welfare

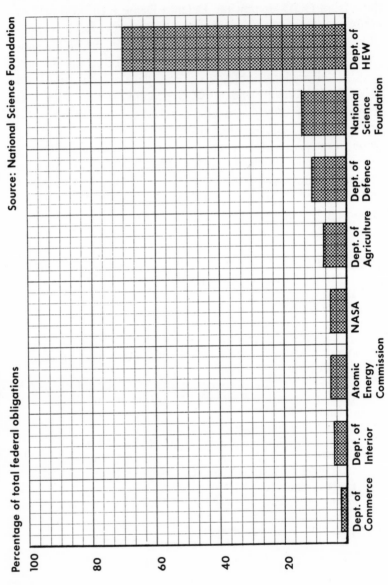

Federal Obligations to Universities and Colleges: 1967.

Source: National Science Foundation

Percentage of total federal obligations

Federal Obligations for Basic Research, by Performer: Fiscal Years 1958 and 1968.

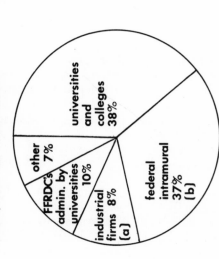

Fiscal year 1958: $335 million

Fiscal year 1968: $2.1 billion (est.)

universities and colleges 38%

other 7%

FFRDC's admin. by universities 10%

industrial firms 8% [a]

federal intramural 37% [b]

universities and colleges 37%

other 7%

FFRDC's admin. by universities 13%

industrial firms 19% [a]

federal intramural 24% [b]

a) Includes federally funded research and development centers (FFRDC's) administered by this sector.

b) Intramural activities cover costs associated with the administration of intramural and extramural programs by federal personnel as well as intramural performance.

Source: National Science Foundation

Office of Education
 Center for Advanced Study of Educational Administration (University of Oregon)
 Center for Research and Development in Higher Education (University of California)
 Center for Research and Development for Learning and Re-Education (University of Wisconsin)
 Center for the Study of Social Organization of Schools and the Learning Process (Johns Hopkins University)
 Center for the Study of the Evaluation of Instructional Programs (University of California)
 Coordination Center for the National Program in Early Childhood Education (University of Illinois)
 Learning Research and Development Center (University of Pittsburgh)
 Research and Development Center in Teacher Education (University of Texas)
 Stanford Center for Research and Development in Teaching (Stanford University)

Atomic Energy Commission
 Ames Laboratory (Iowa State University of Science and Technology)
 Argonne National Laboratory (University of Chicago and Argonne Universities Association)
 Brookhaven National Laboratory (Associated Universities, Inc.)
 Cambridge Electron Accelerator (Harvard University and MIT)
 Lawrence Radiation Laboratory, Berkeley and Livermore (University of California)
 Los Alamos Scientific Laboratory (University of California)
 Oak Ridge Associated Universities
 Plasma Physics Laboratory (Princeton University)
 Princeton-Pennsylvania Accelerator (Princeton and University of Pennsylvania)
 Stanford Linear Accelerator Center (Stanford University)

National Aeronautics and Space Administration
 Jet Propulsion Laboratory (California Institute of Technology)
 Space Radiation Effects Laboratory (College of William and Mary)

National Science Foundation
 Cerro Tololo Inter-American Observatory (Association of Universities for Research in Astronomy, Inc.)

Kitt Peak National Observatory (Association of Universities for Research in Astronomy, Inc.)

National Center for Atmospheric Research (University Corporation for Atmospheric Research)

National Radio Astronomy Observatory (Associated Universities, Inc.)

MILITARY RESEARCH ON CAMPUS

American Universities Among the 500 Contractors Listed According to Net Value of Military Prime Contract Awards for Research, Development, Test and Evaluation Work. Department of Defense—Fiscal Year 1966.

University:	*Value of Contracts:*
Johns Hopkins University	$50,394,000
Massachusetts Institute of Technology	47,308,000
Stanford Research Institute	30,693,000
University of Michigan	19,492,000
Stanford University	18,569,000
Columbia University	16,203,000
University of California	16,149,000
Cornell Aeronautical Laboratory	14,961,000
Illinois Institute of Technology Research Institute	13,952,000
Pennsylvania State University	11,830,000
University of Illinois	10,875,000
Franklin Institute of Pennsylvania	9,117,000
University of Washington	6,434,000
University of Pennsylvania	5,932,000
Cornell University	5,452,000
Syracuse University Research Corporation	5,343,000
George Washington University	5,229,000
University of Denver	5,074,000
Harvard University	4,286,000
University of Texas	4,073,000
New York University	3,929,000
University of Dayton	3,670,000
California Institute of Technology	3,584,000
Princeton University	3,568,000

University:	*Value of Contracts:*
University of Chicago	3,444,000
Ohio State University Research Foundation	3,416,000
Brown University	3,011,000
Northwestern University	2,742,000
Duke University	2,631,000
American University	2,594,000
Brooklyn Polytechnic Institute	2,468,000
University of Maryland	2,314,000
University of Miami	2,139,000
Carnegie Institute of Technology	2,077,000
University of Minnesota	2,061,000
University of Wisconsin	1,928,000
Northeastern University	1,914,000
University of Pittsburgh	1,780,000
New Mexico State University	1,663,000
Purdue Research Foundation	1,629,000
University of Alaska	1,598,000
Research Triangle Institute	1,519,000
Texas A & M Research Foundation	1,397,000
University of Utah	1,367,000
Illinois Institute of Technology	1,305,000
Stevens Institute of Technology	1,271,000
Georgia Tech Research Institute	1,269,000
University of Colorado	1,264,000
Wentworth Institute	1,205,000
Washington University	1,194,000
University of New Mexico	1,143,000
Syracuse University	1,119,000
University of Cincinnati	1,109,000
University of Southern California	1,058,000
University of Rochester	1,056,000
Purdue University	1,046,000
University of North Carolina	954,000
University of Arizona	950,000
Yale University	907,000
Oregon State University	883,000
University of Virginia	865,000
New Mexico School of Mines	845,000
University of Hawaii	787,000

University:	*Value of Contracts:*
University of Rhode Island	770,000
Iowa State University	762,000
Tufts University	759,000
Mellon Institute	758,000
Rensselaer Polytechnic Institute	724,000
University of Florida	690,000
Texas Western College	679,000
Catholic University of America	663,000
State University of New York	656,000
Case Institute of Technology	603,000
Louisiana State University	597,000
Utah State University	563,000
Indiana University	491,000
Rutgers University	483,000
University of Tennessee	471,000
Boston College	449,000
Georgia Institute of Technology	410,000
Emmanuel College	407,000
Temple University	403,000
Notre Dame University	400,000
Western Reserve University	398,000
Dartmouth College	381,000
Rice University	379,000
Ohio State University	378,000
Brandeis University	376,000
University of Alabama	366,000
Oklahoma State University	359,000
Lehigh University	339,000
Missouri University	339,000

The allocation of federal resources from these respective agencies reflects the fact that in 1968 the universities and colleges did 37 percent of all basic research in the United States. An additional 13 percent of the basic research was done in federally funded research and development centers administered by universities and colleges. The combined research performance of the universities and colleges, then, in 1968, was 50 percent of the total.

This, of course, is not to deny the existence of the contractual relations between the DOD and the universities. On the contrary. In 1965 for example, Johns Hopkins University obtained over $50 million in DOD contracts, MIT received better than $47 million, and the Stanford Research Institute (SRI) obtained upwards of $30 million.

Institutions like MIT, California Institute of Technology, and the Stanford Research Institute are awarded contracts for the development of specific pieces of equipment for NASA, the Air Force, etc., competing and operating in much the same way as private industry. In 1969 the University of Illinois (Urbana) was awarded a contract with the DOD to perform a computer simulation of the ABM missile system. As a result the University obtained the largest computer in the world, increasing the total computation capacity of the United States by 25 percent!

Research funds supplied by the federal government are by no means limited to projects in the national and physical sciences. On the contrary, corresponding to the importance of the social and behavioral sciences as instruments for the practical consolidation of the social system, federal funds for research in these areas have also increased. Thus, for example, a report prepared by the US Office of Education observed that without the federal funds supplied the universities most foreign policy center programs would never have been realized:

> The significance of the money granted is all out of proportion to the amounts involved since most universities would have no center programs had they not been subsidized. *Our individual inventories indicate clearly the lack of enthusiasm as well as cash on the part of most college administrations for such programs . . .* [Emphasis added.] [7]

Further, interdisciplinary institutes, some of which have been established and financed by the federal government such as the Institute for Defense Analysis (IDA) combine the attributes of several disciplines to explore effective techniques for domestic counter-insurgency. In 1967, for example, IDA issued a Task Force Report on Science and Technology that included detailed proposals for controlling domestic insurrections:

In a riot or other emergency situations, an emergency communications center, tied to the regular center, must be established to transform a police department from a loose collection of independent units into a cohesive, coordinated force . . . [M]eans must be provided to collect and display, rapidly and continuously, all the varieties of tactical intelligence relating to the location of events and the disposition of forces. The center and selected field units must be equipped with a radio scrambler for greater security . . . The emergency communications center staff must be headed by a commander who can assimilate this information and who has the authority to command the available forces. Contingency plans for situations that might arise and for coordination with other jurisdictions must be developed and stored in a readily accessible form.[8]

The fusion of the state with finance capital, characteristic of advanced imperialist society, is felt first, as Engels observed, in the institutions for intercourse and communication. In the era of the scientific and technological revolution the state assumes a special intimacy with certain strategic institutions of intercourse and communication; in particular, the university.

The tendency toward the state control of higher education—either *de facto* or *de jure*—is sporadic and uneven, and sometimes accompanied by the decentralization (or fragmentation) of non-strategic academic functions (e.g., in the humanities and the arts). There is, too, resistance from the corporate governing boards of both public and private institutions reluctant to relinquish power. Still the national trend can be clearly discerned and the continued fusion between the state and finance capital will render any other direction inefficient and ultimately untenable.

With the state serving as the mechanism through which the university is integrated into the productive process, it begins to assert a direct influence over the material and academic corpus of the university. The federal thrust, sparked by the urgent needs of the scientific-technological revolution, was not accompanied by any prior study of the total impact the state would have on the higher educational system. The largely unplanned intervention—and the uneven, sporadic and unpredictable allocation of federal funds—provoked massive chaos in the structure of the university and in its educational functions.

The emphasis on teaching, for example, was steadily shifted to the more lucrative enterprises of research and publication without adequate preparations. Undergraduate education has been most acutely and adversely affected by this reversal of priorities. As one professor put it:

The wise chairman [of a department] . . . will manipulate his teaching system so as to increase that portion of his budget he may spend to attract academic stars . . . A man becomes an academic star . . . by his ability to publish in accepted journals, read papers before his national association and publish books that are well-received by his well-known colleagues . . . But . . . the standards of professional associations are not directly relevant to teaching, and increasingly these guilds set the standards for college and university appointment and promotion . . .[9]

Even more striking is the inability of colleges and universities to organize and provide curricula which corresponds to reality. This is a reflection of two distinct but causally related events. First, there is the speed with which scientific discoveries can be made, and their results translated into technology. Second, there is the direct social (and socializing) impact of scientific discovery and technological progress. A scientific discovery or technical achievement can cause the rapid transformation of whole systems and processes, as well as the specific modifications more familiar to us.

The level of socialization—i.e., the integration and interdependence of industrial and social processes—now requires a modification in the internal organization of the schools, colleges and departments of the university. That is, it requires an *interdisciplinary* academic structure.

Historically the organization of scientific work in the academy has corresponded to the role of science in the industrial process—from tangential use, to conscious use, to primacy. Two hundred years ago, corresponding to the tangential role of science there were no special departments in any of its particular branches or in general:

> Science was not separate from philosophy, the arts or literature in either organization or personnel. Within the framework of natural philosophy and natural history, the particular fields of physics and chemistry, botany and zoology and mineralogy were clear, but nobody imagined that a man should devote his whole time to them. Indeed almost no one . . . [was a] professional scientist. Many were doctors, lawyers or clergy making their living spending much of their time in ways unconnected with science. . . . [10]

The conscious use of science by the turn of the nineteenth century caused the first internal reorganization in the university. It occurred surprisingly late in the United States. Departments of science were not begun until the second half of the nineteenth century and then it was with reluctance. Harvard offered its first Bachelor of Science degree in 1851; the Yale equivalent was a Bachelor of Philosophy degree offered first in 1852. However:

> The two old foundations kept the B.A. [Bachelor of Arts] degree inviolate and protected it from dilution. At both Yale and Harvard admission standards for candidates for these degrees [in science or philosophy] were lower than for the B.A. degree;

the length of the course of study was three years rather than four; and in both institutions the scientific students were considered second-class citizens . . .[11]

In the decade of the 1860's more than a score of other colleges in the U.S. followed the example of Harvard and Yale.

The first specialized departments in the sciences were not established until the dawn of the twentieth century. But when they arrived they quickly thrust their way into the university. There evolved a system of specialization and professionalism which is today entrenched. It reached a point of diminishing returns by the mid-1950's. The academy must now move to combine an appropriate degree of specialization with an overall interdisciplinary structure.

The intervention of the state provided funds for interdisciplinary institutes in the natural, physical, and social sciences. However, these institutes were superimposed on the specialized departmental apparatus, and have been accompanied by a de-emphasis of undergraduate teaching and an astronomical increase in the number of students. The result is internal anarchy.

The internal crisis is compounded by the social context in which the university exists. In particular, as the university is further integrated into the industrial process, and its relationship to the state is further cemented, it begins to assume certain anarchistic tendencies characteristic of capitalist relations of production; albeit, with the particular nuance of academe. The academy, for example, suffers the trauma of overproduction; but it overproduces people instead of cars. The "overproduction" of Ph.D.'s in all branches of the academic sciences is a case in point. During the last ten years there has been over a 60 percent increase in the number of universities offering Ph.D. programs. This corresponded to the projected (but inaccurately projected) demands for college teachers by the 1970's. The number of doctorates conferred each year grows steadily. In 1958 only 8,800 doctorates were conferred in the United States. In 1969 there were almost 23,000.

The universities and colleges employ over 65 percent of all Ph.D. holders in teaching and/or research. Up until very recently there was a heavy demand for more teachers and researchers. The situation is now reversing itself. It is forecast that by 1980 there will be 350,000 science Ph.D's in the country and a utilization level of between 275,000 and 300,000.[12]

Philosophically the bourgeoisie conceives of capitalism as a perfectly natural and rational system. The capitalist state then is seen as a pragmatic and primarily negative agent. The state is merely the organ to manage and supervise the prevailing (natural) social and economic processes. Politically its functions are negative in the sense that it must moderate and contain the antagonisms and clashes which it is assumed, are natural and inherent in any human society. As these (natural) human clashes intensify, the coercive power of the state, must (unfortunately) increase.

The scientific-technological revolution, however, suggests that the state must assume exactly opposite functions. It cannot be the negative force of coercion and conformity. It must become the positive agent of diversity and innovation.

The imperialist state in both philosophical origin and contemporary reality fulfills neither requisite function of the scientific-technological revolution very well. Attempts at social planning stagger under the uncertainties of private competition and the tendency toward over-production. They are turned inside out and upside down with the introduction of *planned obsolescence*. The *private* appropriation of *socially* produced wealth cripples the state's financial capabilities to provide necessary social services and operations.*

* This refers to two things: 1) the acute crisis in the cities where there

The anarchy of capitalist production ultimately evokes chaos in many spheres of social life. In the era of the scientific-technological revolution, the imperialist state does not expedite anything. On the contrary, it confounds everything.

For the *primary* feature of the imperialist state remains: it is the instrument of class domination and oppression. It discovers in science and technology hitherto unknown means of coercion and manipulation. As the organ which subsidizes, organizes, directs, and controls it introduces new techniques of social oppression (and repression), and new methods of economic exploitation (and penetration).

But the imperialist state becomes internally at odds with itself. Its coercive and oppressive social (and economic) functions actively inhibit the scientific progress it must encourage. The anachronistic and anarchistic capitalist relations of production—the private appropriation of socially produced wealth—which the capitalist state must seek to preserve, obstruct the technological development it is simultaneously called upon to project.

It is precisely in the arena of academic planning that the state's inability to perform the new functions assigned by the scientific-technological revolution are most apparent. For it is in its inability to be the active social prognostic, on both the national and local level, that it further inhibits scientific and social progress.

Since 1967 the *rate of increase* of federal funds for Research and Development has steadily declined. In particular budget categories there has been an *actual* decrease in federal funds from the previous years. The total federal support of higher education increased by some $2 billion between 1963 and

---

is a lack of profitability in public projects, and a lack of sufficient funds to meet social needs of housing, transportation, health, education, and so forth; and 2) the inability of the system to meet the *social needs of production* resulting from the level of socialization, e.g., the crisis of the railroads, of the post office, of the airlines, of the telephone communications, and so forth.

1967. *The yearly growth, however, had slowed from 42 percent and 32 percent in 1965 and 1966 respectively, to 9 percent in 1967.* Meanwhile in the same span of time (1964 to 1967) federal support for non-science programs rose from $96 million to $987 million. As a percent of total federal obligations these non-science funds rose from 6 to 30 percent.

Two trends are discernible: 1) while total federal expenditures to higher education since 1967 have remained relatively constant, the rate of increase of these funds has declined precipitously in general, and in the academic sciences in particular. 2) In general the proportional rate of federal expenditures for nonscience academic projects has increased, while the rate of increase for the academic sciences continues to decline.*

While on the whole the absolute funds for the academic sciences may increase slightly, they do not keep pace with the spiraling costs of research. Moreover, the budget cuts hit certain agencies more drastically than others. One writer for *Science* magazine explained what he called the "budget paradox":

> The explanation of how a level budget can cause problems lies partly in the fact that the cost of research keeps going up and therefore more money is needed just to keep even, and partly in the fact that this year's [1968] budget crunch has fallen more heavily on some agencies and scientists than others.[13]

Agencies as large as the Department of Defense and the Atomic Energy Commission have been able to protect their research budgets by making cuts in other programs; whereas the cuts in the NASA budget, for example, can only result in a reduction in its assistance to universities. Likewise, budget

---

* This statistical trend probably reflects an increase in federal expenditures for the construction of new schools, the development of professional and technical training programs, etc., spurred by the demand for narrowly trained but highly skilled technical workers.

cuts or even levellings-off in the National Science Foundation and the National Institutes of Health where research is the prime activity leave them relatively helpless. They in turn are forced to cut their assistance to the universities.

Studies in late 1969 indicated that the federal budget cuts were beginning to affect the growth of campus computer operations. A survey of some three dozen major colleges and universities earlier that year discovered that:

. . . the increase in computer operating expenses at these institutions will drop from 29 percent a year during the period 1965 to 1968 to 13 percent a year between 1969 and 1971. In part these figures represent an anticipated levelling-off in the growth of computer facilities after a decade of rapid expansion, but many of these universities also expect computer use by federally sponsored projects to rise less rapidly under tight budgets.[14]

Since 1940, total expenditures for the public universities and colleges have *exceeded* the total expenditures for the private universities. That national trend continues in spite of the enormous budgets of certain private institutions like Harvard and Columbia. This tendency has been exaggerated by the post '67 budget cuts. As one administrator explained, the private universities by-and-large rely on their strong and well-financed graduate and research programs "to attract and hold the faculty." These are the very programs which are most dependent upon federal funds. In this way the private institutions feel the current budget squeeze the hardest—relative to prevailing standards. This administrator warned that ". . . The lag in federal money and spiraling costs are jeopardizing the survival of U.S. private universities." [15]

Since 1967 increasing numbers of scientists have found themselves stranded in the middle of projects, or facing uncertain futures. This financial ambiguity contributes to a decline in scientific inquiry, by making it increasingly difficult to plan for the future.[16] More importantly, the budget cuts are illustrative of the lack of *social* planning which reflects *human* priority. What it does reflect is the calculated shift to specific military priorities.[17]

The 1968 fiscal budget of the National Institutes of Health (NIH) was $1.93 billion. Under the Nixon administration the budget was cut in 1969 to $1.64 billion. Most academicians seem to agree that the main effect is on the medical schools and on the output of future doctors, teachers, and researchers. The president of the American Medical Colleges reported that these schools get upwards of 40 percent of their total income from federal research and training grants. He stated that the nine schools are now "teetering on the edge of insolvency."

Summarizing the effects of the budget cuts to the NIH, one journal reported:

> To save some $9 million a year, five major programs to attack chronic and crippling diseases—heart disease, stroke, cancer, arthritis, diabetes, neurological and sensory diseases, and lung diseases —are to be phased out. To save $4 million, 19 of 93 clinical research centers are to be abolished. To save $400,000 the world famous National Heart Institute program to study factors contributing to heart disease is being ended . . .[18]

The National Advisory Council on Education Professions Development, in preparing its annual report for 1969– 1970 issued a five-page Memorandum to the President and summarized its opinion of the national state of higher education: "Everywhere the mood appears to be one of cutting back—withdrawing—seeing how little we can get along with; in short, a steady retreat from the bold plans launched several years ago . . ." [19] One professor of chemistry referring to the effects of the budget cuts spoke bluntly: "We are witnessing the mindless dismantling of the American scientific enterprise." [20]

The national uncertainties have further complicated the dilemma of individual states in their efforts to predict academic needs and allocate appropriate resources.

Faced with a flood of federal funds, vast functional changes, enormous leaps in student enrollment, the competition for funds between public and private institutions, and no clear delineation of institutional responsibilities, states began in the late 1940's to consciously project the needs of their educational systems. This occurred also in California, and its Master Plan for Higher Education, adopted in 1960, is a prototype of those proposed or adopted in several other states.

In 1948 the California State Legislature authorized a special committee—the Strayer Committee—which had been established by the Liaison Committee of the Regents of the University of California and the State Board of Education, to study the development of higher education. The Committee published its recommendations in its *Report of a Survey of the Needs of California in Higher Education* about a year later. Its central and most far-reaching proposal was that the *de facto* functional roles of the junior colleges, the state colleges and the university were to be given the force of law in the future higher educational scheme:

> The unskilled and semi-skilled [workers] learn what they need to know by pick-up methods. Skilled workers become such through apprenticeship or by mastering courses on the high school level. Technical programs have in California long been regarded as the province of the two-year junior colleges, while professional training is the province of the university. It is the level between the technical training of the junior colleges and the professional and research departments of the university towards which the occupational curricula of the state colleges are pointed.[21]

Within a few years the state agencies again authorized a study, and in 1955 the McConnell Report, titled *A Restudy of the Needs of California in Higher Education* was issued:

> [It] strongly endorsed the principles of different functions. While recognizing "the necessity of a considerable overlapping in the purposes and programs in the state colleges and universities," it

nevertheless concluded that the principle of differentiation was sound: "It is recommended that the junior colleges continue to take particular responsibility for technical curriculums, the state colleges for occupational curriculums, and the University of California for graduate and professional education and research." [22]

The Master Plan for Higher Education, 1960–1975, embodied in law as the Donahoe Act of 1960, derived essentially from these preliminary studies. It revised sections of the California State Constitution (Article IX), to establish the functional differentiation of the three *public* sectors of higher education,* and accordingly provide for their governance and finance.

The junior colleges were maintained as part of the Public School System under the control of the State Board of Education, each to be governed by local boards

selected for the purpose from each district maintaining one or more junior colleges . . . Public junior colleges shall offer instruction through but not beyond the 14th grade level including but not limited to, one or more of the following: (a) standard collegiate courses for transfer to higher institutions, (b) vocational-technical fields leading to employment and (c) general, or liberal arts courses . . .** [23]

The State Colleges were to be unified under central administration control

for the first time, . . . administered by a body corporate known as the Trustees . . . with number, term of appointment and powers

* The Donahoe Act *does not* restrict the private colleges and universities in California, e.g., Stanford or the California Institute of Technology, etc.
** The junior colleges, as part of the Public School System, are largely financed through local property taxes, receiving a very small percentage of their funds from either the state or federal governments. By this constitutional provision the Donahoe Act froze the junior colleges into a financial strait-jacket. Most of the federal funds are matching grants for EOP projects, and the state funds are computed as a percentage of ADA (Average Daily Attendance).

closely paralleling those of the Regents . . . The state colleges shall have as their primary function the provision of instruction in the liberal arts and sciences and in professions and applied fields which require more than two years of collegiate education, and teacher education, both for undergraduate students and graduate students through the master's degree. . . . Faculty research, using facilities provided for and consistent with the primary function of the state college is authorized.[24]

The University of California remained intact. Its functions and prerogatives were made explicit:

The University shall provide instruction in the liberal arts and sciences, and in the professions, including teacher education, and shall have *exclusive jurisdiction* over training for the professions including but not by way of limitation, dentistry, law, medicine, veterinary medicine and graduate architecture. The University shall have the *sole authority in public higher education* to award the doctor's degree in all fields of learning, *except that* it may agree with the state colleges to allow joint doctor's degrees in selected fields. The university shall be the primary state supported academic agency for research.[25]

The admissions requirements to the junior colleges, state colleges, and the university maintained and reinforced this pattern of functional differentiation. The junior colleges are open to any California resident with a high school diploma (from an accredited high school); the state colleges are open to all California high school graduates in the top one-third of all graduating seniors *in the state* (not in their own schools); and the university is open to all California high school graduates in the top one-sixth of all seniors in the state.*

* By 1969 these figures were purely theoretical. The budget cuts on both state and federal levels and the rate of expansion being above what was anticipated, tens of thousands of eligible students in California were denied admission to both the university and the state colleges. Despite the sky-rocketing enrollment figures, 20 percent of the eligible students who applied for admission to the state colleges in the fall of 1969 were denied admission. National figures reflect the same thing. The percentage of college applicants rejected has risen from 25 percent in 1965 to 43 percent in 1969. In the junior colleges, the

The statistical data in 1964 suggested the pattern of class and racial discrimination in California higher education: [27]

	Median Family Income of of Students	% of students with family income over $14,000 a year	% of students Black and Chicano
Junior Colleges	$8,800	18%	14%
State Colleges	$10,000	21%	6%
University of California	$12,000	39%	3%

Supplemental data indicated that if the Master Plan affected anything, it tended to reinforce the discriminatory patterns. By 1967, for example, there was an *actual decline* in the percentage of Black and Chicano students in the University of California and in the state colleges—in the university from 3 percent in 1964 to under 2 percent in 1967; in the state colleges from 6 percent in 1964 to 5 percent in 1967.

The total enrollment of Black and Chicano students increased slightly in all branches of California public higher education in 1968–1969 due in large measure to Economic Opportunities (EOP) and Black and Ethnic Studies Programs begun on many campuses, largely a result of student demands. However, the threatened and real budget cuts on state and federal levels are hurting, and seriously limiting or preventing their growth. A steady upward trend in the proportion of Black and Chicano enrollment cannot be expected.

Additional manifestations of class and racial discrimination are discerned by comparing the average institutional expendi-

---

drop-out rates are extraordinarily high. So that while technically all high school graduates are eligible, a variety of factors, many of them financial, prevent the students from completing even their junior college courses. The Unruh Report for example, noted "a very substantial increase in the attrition rates within the first two years of junior college" [26] Additionally, a majority of junior college students are part-time. In 1965, for example, of the total enrollment of 481,831 in the California junior colleges, 288,916 were part-time.

tures per student (1966/67) in each of the public sectors of higher education in California: [28]

	Expenditures per year	Expenditures during Average Period of Attendance
Junior Colleges	$837	$1,000
State Colleges	$1,140	$3,000
University of California	$2,230	$6,000

Further illustrative of class discrimination is the allocation of financial resources by the state government for each sector. While the junior colleges experience the highest enrollment, expected to total 858,000 full and part-time students by 1975 (or 60 percent of all students in California), they receive the smallest percentage of financial support from the state. Meanwhile, the University of California with the smallest percentage of students receives nearly 50 percent of all state funds allocated for public higher education.

From virtually every vantage point it can be seen that the effect of the California Master Plan has been to institutionalize and reinforce the historic, *de facto* class and racial discrimination in the educational system in general, and in higher education in particular. The crisis is again compounded by the erroneous projections of the Master Plan, even from a purely technical point of view, as evidenced by the recent legislative stirrings, and the deluge of corrective statistics, reports, studies, and proposals.

Attempts at academic planning are still further complicated by the fact that the private universities and colleges are not subject to the relevant provisions of the state constitution, or to the Donahoe Act. Nevertheless, both public and private institutions compete with each other for government funds, contractual advantage, private endowments and so forth. The chairman of the original committee to draft the California Master Plan conveyed the spirit of academic discord:

The main struggles have been between [the institutions] themselves vying for advantage, favor and finance. At times these segments have sought or found common ground. At other times, and more characteristically, they have been vying vigorously for their own interests often with not much evidence to support the idea of a commonly respected profession, manifesting bitter animosity, charges and counter claims . . .[29]

The problems encountered in academic planning are fourfold. First, part of the internal anarchy within each institution results from the imposition of a necessary interdisciplinary method on a specialized departmental structure accompanied by a decline in teaching priority and an astronomical increase in the student population. The anarchy precipitates and reinforces the bureaucratic and hierarchical structure of the academy. For while anarchy and bureaucracy are opposites, they are *dialectical* opposites, the former contributing to the rise of bureaucracy, and the bureaucracy reinforcing the anarchistic tendencies. This wreaks havoc with efforts to define budget categories, determine the rational allocation of resources, and eliminate repetitive research and teaching programs. Second, the state governments exercise exceedingly limited control over federal budgetary decisions, while federal funds represent a large portion of its resources for higher education. Moreover, there is a lack of consistency in the federal allocations for specific budget categories. Third, the values and priorities of the imperialist state are superimposed on the academic structure institutionalizing its worst racist, exploitative, and oppressive features, and further aggravating unjust and unbearable social conditions, especially for Black and Chicano people. Fourth, the academy, in both the public and private sector, as a constituent part of the industrial process, assumes many of the competitive characteristics of capitalist enterprise, which give rise to a tendency toward the over-production of scientists, social scientists, professional workers, and engineers, and lock the institutions into a perpetual state of intramural and intercollegiate hostilities.

The scientific-technological revolution also renders *prognosis the prerequisite of educational relevance*. This, in a purely technical sense, given the rate of scientific discovery and the speed with which it is translated into technology. This also in the social sense given the direct social (and socializing) impact of scientific progress.

Social prognosis *is* employed by the imperialist state; but its basic necessities and priorities are anti-human. That is, the prognostic function of the state becomes by-in-large "negative social planning" (which is a contradiction in terms). We experience the *planned obsolescence* of commodities; the *planned disruption* of needed research; the *planned enforcement* of class and racial inequities. There is then the explicit denial and the overt destruction of the unity between scientific-technical progress, and its redeeming social value. *In essence, there is a tendency toward planned insanity*.

The intramural and intercollegiate hostilities, the irreconcilable conflicts between academic need and imperialist priority—in short, the internal contradictions of the social order as manifested in the functions of the academy—approach their new apex. Prognosis is the prerequisite of educational relevance. Educational relevance requires the introduction of an interdisciplinary academic structure (with appropriate degrees of specialization). The interdisciplinary academic structure rests upon the recognition of an organic unity between all productive and social forces. That unity must be *consciously* projected, and therefore it depends upon the prognostic and innovative functions of the state. The imperialist state as it seeks to organize, subsidize, direct, and control the academy imposes upon it anti-human and anti-social functions and values. The resolution of these contradictions is the source of a requisite revolution to humanize the objectives of the university, liberate its faculty and students, and inspire an intellectual Renaissance.

6 ALIENATION

The history of the United States is replete with examples of student activism and faculty dissent. Intellectual ferment has traditionally accompanied social crisis—from the abolitionist movement to Reconstruction; from Populism to the anti-imperialist leagues, to the women's suffrage movement and the resistance to world wars and fascism.

The fact of rebellion then, does not in itself describe the new qualities of the insurgent sixties. Rather, it is the persistence of insurgency, its geographic scope, social breadth and political depth that suggest a new quality. The academic rebellion could not be contained in its embryonic stage (as had been true in the past) because of a combination of interrelated social factors: the general systemic crisis—in particular the escalation of the war in Vietnam, and the worsening domestic crises of racism and poverty; and the simultaneous emergence of the university as an integral part of the production process.

For as the university becomes a constituent part of the production process its relationship to society is changed. The university becomes an essential instrument for waging war in general, and for waging the war in Vietnam in particular. This fact forces thousands of intellectuals and students to confront the politics of war in a new way. Likewise, the university becomes an essential instrument for the practical consolidation of the system. This fact forces thousands of intellectuals and students to confront the politics of society—and the politics of social change—in a new way.

The effect of this change in the relationship of the university to society may be posed this way: the emergence of the university as an integral part of the production .process creates a situation in which, for the first time since the division of mental from manual labor, the alienation of the intellectuals and the students is rooted in the material conditions of their existence. That is, the academic rebellion is no longer simply a response to moments of social injustice, or a movement for abstract moral values, as it has tended to be historically. On the contrary, the rebellion is more and more an expression of the growing alienation of students and intellectuals from mental labor itself, from teaching and research.

From the Marxist view the quality of a worker's relationship to the productive process is identical whether he is selling manual or mental labor. For in either case the worker is reduced to a commodity. From the point of view of bourgeois political economy, writes Marx: "The part of capital laid out for wages is no longer in the least distinguished . . . from the part of capital laid out for raw materials . . ."[1] Indeed, "These labourers, who must sell themselves piecemeal, are a commodity like every other article of commerce, and are consequently exposed to all the vicissitudes of competition, to all the fluctuations of the market . . ."[2] This is the plight of an increasing proportion of social scientists, professional workers, scientists, and engineers in the U.S. today whether employed directly in industry, or in the university (now be-

coming a constituent part of the production process). It is
the explicit future of the students. Professional, social, technical and scientific workers are overproduced, underemployed,
misemployed, and unemployed. Increasingly they must sell
their intellectual and technical skills whenever, wherever and
however the market permits.[3]

Marxists have long considered engineers and technical
workers employed in industry to be a part of the working
class. The point here is this: as the university is tied more and
more *into* the production process, the tendency is for the
intellectuals within the university to become a constituent
part of the working class. Given the different forms of intellectual labor this process is varied and uneven. Thus the relationship of scientists and engineers to the production process—even as they work within the university—is more obvious.
The social scientists within the university, on the other hand,
appear to assume a dual class position because of the specifically ideological nature of their work.

The social scientists within the university remain as an
integral part of the superstructure for the university itself
is a part of it. However, they are also attached to the base of
the social system (the production process) by virtue of the
fact that the university is becoming a constituent part of it.

The impact of this interaction between the base and the
superstructure on the university is such that the nature of the
social scientists' work is being qualitatively transformed, and
they are increasingly thrust toward a working class posture
in their day-to-day existence. Their study of man is highly
technical and routinized; man himself is reified—i.e. made
into an object. Further, the social scientists along with the
rest of the intelligentsia assume a commodity status, and their
employability is subject to all the fluctuations of the academic market. The tendency in highly industrialized countries is for the entire intelligentsia to be dragged, kicking and

screaming as it were, into becoming a constituent part of the working class.

As the university becomes a part of the productive process there is a dramatic transformation in the social conditions of labor within the academy; that is, the industrialization and socialization of the total academic enterprise. Consequently, the intellectual begins to experience, in a distinct but analogous way, the interpenetrating aspects of the alienation of labor as described by Marx: alienation from the product of his labor; alienation from the act of his labor (or from the process of producing); and the alienation of man from man (and man from himself).

Fundamental to Marx's view of alienation was his consideration of man primarily and essentially as *producer:* "Man can be distinguished from animals by consciousness, by religion or anything else you like. They themselves begin to distinguish themselves from animals as soon as they begin to *produce* their means of subsistence." [4] For Marx, *productive* labor is necessarily a conscious process—and this distinguishes man's labor from the instinctive behavior of other animals:

We pre-suppose labour in a form that stamps it as exclusively human. A spider conducts operations that resemble those of a weaver, and a bee puts to shame many an architect in the construction of her cells. But what distinguishes the worst architect from the best of bees is this, that the architect raises his structure in imagination before he erects it in reality. At the end of every labour-process, we get a result that already existed in the imagination of the labourer at its commencement. He not only effects a change of form in the material on which he works, but he also realises a purpose of his own that gives the law to his modus operandi, and to which he must subordinate his will. [5]

For Marx, then, only man can suffer alienation.

From this definitive view of man *as a worker,* Marx and

Engels continue: "By producing their means of subsistence men are indirectly producing their actual material life . . ." [6] In this way Marx sees an organic relationship between the nature of man's work and his own nature; hence the organic link between man's work and the conscious ends he sets for himself in his work:

Labor is . . . a process in which both man and nature participate, and in which man of his own accord starts, regulates, and controls the material reactions between himself and nature. He opposes himself to nature as one of her own forces, setting in motion arms and legs, head and hands, the natural forces of his body, in order to appropriate nature's productions in a form adapted to his own wants. By thus acting on the external world and changing it, he at the same time changes his own nature. [7]

In the capitalist scheme "alienated man loses his *being,* his essence, which is the self-conscious pursuit of ends that he realizes in his work. He has become an object . . ." [8] A vivid illustration of this view of man as an object (a commodity) is available from a nineteenth-century devotee of Adam Smith, who, if we can say nothing else about him, is refreshingly honest in his appraisal:

By the infirmity of human nature it happens, that the more skillful the workman, the more self-willed and intractable he is apt to become, and, of course, the less fit a component of a mechanical system, in which, by occasional irregularities, he may do great damage to the whole. The grand object therefore of modern manufacture is, through union of capital and science, to reduce the task of his work people to the exercise of vigilance and dexterity—faculties, *when concentrated in one process,* speedily brought to perfection in the young . . . [9]

The whole point of modern industry, then, is to reduce the worker, as Marx said, to becoming "the flesh-and-blood appendage to a steel machine . . ."

Marx describes the alienation of the worker from the product of his labor this way:

> . . . the more the worker produces, the less he has to consume; the more value he creates the more worthless and unworthy he becomes; the better shaped his product, the more misshapen he is; . . . the more powerful the work, the more powerless he becomes; the more intelligence the work has, the more witless the worker and the more he becomes a slave of nature . . .[10]

This brilliant juxtaposition is another way of looking at the central contradiction of capitalist society—the *private* appropriation of *socially produced* wealth. For the product of the workers' labor is privately appropriated and therefore the social purposes or uses of that product are determined by the capitalist who has appropriated it and not by the workers who have created it. It is in this way that the system ruptures the organic link between man's work and the conscious ends he sets for himself in his work.

The intellectuals, now becoming a constituent part of the working class, experience this aspect of alienation. The university and college is the social institution in which millions of young people are trained to perform certain (usually specific) future productive or social functions. The teacher is no longer teaching. The teacher is engaged in the production of the future means of production (or in the production of the future social and professional workers). That is, the teacher is processing, molding, fashioning and perfecting a specific product—a B.S. in chemistry, a statistician, a laboratory technician, a mechanical engineer, a teacher, a social psychologist.

Moreover, the relationship is not of one or two students to one or two teachers, but one student to scores of teachers, and one teacher to thousands of students. As a result of the specialization and socialization of the academic enterprise a highly developed division of labor emerges within the university. Both student and teacher experience a loss of identity, a sense of depersonalization.

The student *is* what Mario Savio rhetorically called the "raw material"; [11] and the teacher is reduced to the convoluted appendage to an academic machine, fashioning a portion of the final (human) product.

The description may seem unduly harsh and exaggerated. *It is exaggerated,* primarily because it doesn't simultaneously take into account the intellectuals' spontaneous resistance to such industrial-imperial barbarism, a resistance in large measure reflecting the humanist tradition which constitutes an integral part of the intellectual enterprise. But the exaggeration is useful for it exposes the quintessence of the bourgeois perspective so often disguised in a liberal myth of "inevitability." [12]

In the education industry the alien object of the teachers' labor is the student. He is made into an object, a future commodity. Under capitalism the alienation of man from himself, and man from man, becomes a direct, inescapable consequence of teaching.

The object of the teacher's alienation—the product of his labor—once an inanimate object, is now quite animate and *reciprocates in kind.* The alienation of the teacher from the student (and from teaching, the "act of producing") rooted in the very nature of their relationship to each other, and their relationship to the productive process, necessarily engenders the alienation of the student from the teacher (and from learning—the "process of being produced").

The second aspect of alienation is to be found in the "process of production, in the producing activity itself . . ." If the object of labor is alien to the worker, then Marx insists, the whole process of production is necessarily alien and oppressive: "How could the worker stand in an alien relationship to the product of his activity if he did not alienate himself from himself in the very act of production. After all, the product is only the résumé of activity, of production . . ." [13]

The methods and means of teaching, the whole structure of the industry, while influenced by the faculty (and to a far lesser extent by the students) is determined by the governing boards of trustees, the corporate foundations and the imperialist state. The capitalist not only dictates the aims of the teachers' work; he also determines the means and methods, the conditions of their labor.

Consequently, the intellectual not only assumes a commodity-status; but in a correlative way, his work becomes *vocational*. It tends to lose its challenge, its evocative, avocational qualities, degenerating into a mechanical, repetitious and dull exercise. A basic source of tension within the university is that it can no longer be *characterized* as an educational institution. Instead it takes on the characteristics of a center for vocational training in both a programmatic and spiritual sense.

One distinguished literary scholar observed the routinization and standardization of academic life this way: "Education [is] the process of helping people develop the capacity to deal with information, to become personally integrated, to release creative potential. The routines of schooling and the apparatus of crediting and certifying not only fail to achieve such goals, but make their achievement more difficult." [14]

This is true, and the contradictions can (and should) be posed more concretely and categorically. For the problem is not rooted in the standardization of courses, or in the apparatus of crediting and certifying *per se*. These are reflections of the *commodization* of the intellectual (and the student). For example, to develop a means of distinguishing lesser and greater ability of students in particular fields of study is not *inherently* oppressive. In fact, it can be constructive if its purpose is to channel intellectual resources, and redirect energies, not competitively, but in ways that are socially useful. However, in the social context of ruthless competition, of "rugged individualism," of intellectual worker-as-object, it is positively destructive of the educational enterprise.

Education is, at least in part, liberation and articulation: "Liberation above all, from irrational fears and prejudice; from ignorance; and from mental oppression by traditions, by conformity pressure or by dictators or demagogues. By articulation I mean acquiring mastery of the arts of reading and writing, and of the crafts of logical (including mathematical) and scientific analysis." [15]

The entire structure of the "industrialized" university is increasingly violative of its educational function. The academic pressures and commitments toward intellectual conformity, the petty personal feuds, the fearful intramural competition for available funds tend to overwhelm the institution, obscuring and finally destroying its educational purpose. Pressures on the graduate student are particularly acute and therefore offer an especially devastating example of university life:

When he enters graduate school the young political scientist [for example] . . . knows that there are certain names which win favorable responses from certain professors. He noticed this in college where a well-placed "Dahl" or "Almond" was easily worth an A. The first two years of graduate school devoted to course work, become an elaboration of the importance of those names. . . . Course work is followed by comprehensive examinations. . . . A comprehensive examination is a form of human activity in which people with a vested interest in doing things a certain way obtain assurances from other people that if permitted to do these things, they too will do them in the same way. . . . Knowledge is the degree to which the person can manipulate with ease the names of the masters and the ideas associated with those names. . . .

. . . University life is departmental life. [The graduate student's] senior professor called his attention to an opening at Blank University. . . . After meeting with the tenured members of that department and saying to them substantially the same thing he said in his comprehensive examination, he is offered a three-year contract as an assistant professor with a nine-hour teaching load. Now a variety of choices is open to him. He can publish (over the next six years) one book and three articles, or six articles, or two books. . . . If he didn't know it before, he learns quickly enough that publication, and only publication, counts in his career. . . .[16]

While this description, again, may seem unduly harsh, it is, nonetheless, an accurate reflection of the sentiments of thousands of graduate students in especially the larger, more prestigious institutions; and those sentiments reflect the basic reality of university life. This second aspect of alienation, rooted in the conditions of labor (the methods and means of teaching, and therefore of learning), necessarily interacts with and deepens the first aspect of alienation—the alienation of the worker (the teacher) from his product (the student); and therefore the alienation of the student from the teacher.

Many students and teachers, as yet unaware of the *common, interpenetrating* source of their alienation, have tended to do battle with each other, responding to what superficially appeared as the source of their antagonism. The Marxian theory of alienation transposed to this new sphere of production exposes in an astonishingly literal way a principle source of conflict and discord in the university. Again, Marx's description is profound:

The externalization of the worker in his product [in this case the student] means not only that his work becomes an object, an *external existence,* but also that it exists *outside himself,* independently, alien, an autonomous power, opposed to him. The life he has given to the object [the student] confronts him as hostile and alien. . . .[17]

The intellectual's alienation from his labor is not confined to his academic function as a teacher (or student). Equally oppressive is his common alienation from scientific and social research.

The late physiologist Robert Hodes offered a useful definition of science: "1) Science is ordered knowledge; 2) The knowledge encompassed concerns natural phenomena; and 3) Science deals with interrelationships between phenomena or process, thus indicating a *dynamic* body of knowledge . . ." [18]

The scientific method requires the recognition and formulation of a problem; the collection of data through observation and/or experiment; [19] the formulation of an hypothesis; and the testing and confirmation of that hypothesis. The scientific method requires the verification of theory in practice, and ". . . theory suggests practice, which in turn suggests further or better theory and vice-versa . . ." [20]

The scientific method embodies a particular philosophical conception of science. This philosophical view assumes that the collection of data—that is to say, quantitative analysis— is essential to science, but not its totality. It is only one dimension of scientific inquiry: observation, computation, codification. The collection of data necessarily results in only a partitive consideration of reality. [21] The fragments of this scientific reality must then be placed in the philosophical realm for unification and evaluation:

As soon as the sciences wish to understand themselves, as soon as they wish to grasp the purpose and significance of their own doings, they have to turn to philosophy which is the supreme satisfaction of the theoretical mind and its tendency to comprehend everything in a unity . . . [22]

The scientific method, then, not only embodies a particular philosophical conception of science. The scientific method also defines one aspect of the relationship between science and philosophy. Without perception (observation) there can be no conception (evaluation and unification). Without conception the perception is without scientific value. This may be considered the *naturalistic* aspect of the interpenetration of science and philosophy.

Having established the relationship between science and philosophy in the naturalistic realm, a more urgent question presents itself. Is there an equally essential interpenetration of science and philosophy in the social realm which, if ignored, undermines the viability of scientific inquiry itself? Dominant trends in the scientific and philosophical communities in the United States today reject any such interpenetration, and consider science to be neutral, standing aloof from all social issues and antagonisms. We think that this conception of science is a major source of tension and conflict in the university community, though we recognize the extreme complexities involved in trying to define the relationship between science and philosophy in the social realm.

In the naturalistic sphere science is neutral. That is, scientific (natural) laws exist independent of our will, or whether or not we have discovered them, and they will operate with equal force in any and all social systems. Marx emphasized that ". . . It is absolutely impossible to transcend the laws of nature. What *can* change in historically different circumstances is only the *form* in which the laws express themselves." [23]

Does science, however, as *distinct* from natural law exist in and of itself? It does not, and cannot. For science is created by man. Science is the highest form of human labor, and as with all forms of labor, it is created by man in order to facilitate, organize, systematize his mastery over nature. In this connection it is also important to recognize the specific Marxian concept of nature:

It is the socio-historical character of Marx's concept of nature which distinguishes it from the outset. Marx considered nature to be "the primary source of all instruments and objects of labour," i.e., he saw nature from the beginning in relation to human activity. All other statements about nature, whether of a speculative, epistemological or scientific kind, already presuppose social practice, the ensemble of man's technologico-economic modes of appropriation.[24]

Science, as a form of human labor, bound up with man's mastery over nature, is and always has been bound up with man's social development, and the organization of society.

It is impossible to divorce science from man's social development just as it is impossible to divorce any form of labor from it social context.

Labor performed under exploitative social conditions presents two qualities at the same time: it is both creative and alienating, both humanistic and anti-human. This is equally true of scientific labor. Marx continually emphasized that ". . . men must remain in a continuous process of exchange with nature in order to reproduce their life. Men change the "forms of the materials of nature," in a manner which is the more appropriate to their needs, the better they know those forms. The process of knowledge is therefore not a purely theoretical, internal process. *It stands in the service of life.* Marx saw nothing but an expression of man's self-alienation in the notion that knowledge has a self-sufficient existence, cut off from life, as presented by all contemplative philosophy . . ." [25]

Science as labor then is essentially creative, though its creative qualities may be distorted in an exploitative social context. Insofar as science is the highest form of human labor whose purpose is the mastery of nature "in the service of life" it is essentially rational and essentially humanistic, though at times and in a particular social context it may serve irrational and anti-human ends. The social context in this regard is the decisive factor. Reason, for example, as an intrinsic quality of science may be distorted in an irrational social context. That is to say, reason should not be defined solely in terms of logic. If there is an irrational (social) premise, and/or an irrational (social) goal, an internally logical sequence can be presented, but this still constitutes an irrational whole.

The humanistic essence of science may be viewed in the following way, according to Marx:

> . . . the natural sciences have penetrated all the more *practically* into human life, through their transformation of industry. They have prepared the emancipation of humanity, even though their immediate effect may have been to accentuate the dehumanizing of man. *Industry* is the real historical relation of Nature, and thus of the natural sciences, to man. Consequently, if industry is conceived as an *esoteric* form of the realization of the *essential human faculties,* one is able to grasp also the *human* essence of Nature, or the *natural* essence of man. The natural sciences will then abandon their . . . idealist orientation, and will become the basis of a *human* science, just as they have already become—though in an alienated form—the basis of a really human life. *One* basis for life and another for *science* is *a priori* a falsehood. Nature, as it develops in human history, in the genesis of human society, is the *real* nature of man; thus Nature, as it develops through industry, though in an *alienated* form, is truly *anthropological* Nature.[26]

From this view of science as the highest form of labor, we may suggest the relationship between science and philosophy in the social realm. The first and principal question of philosophy should be: "What is man? If we think about it we see that when we ask what man *is,* we are really asking what can man *become,* that is, can man dominate his own destiny, can he remake himself, can he create his own life?" [27] This represents the social aspect of the interpenetration between science and philosophy: one the instrument for satisfying the quest of the other; and the philosophical quest the motive force of science.

Scientific discovery—i.e., that which changes our conception of nature and therefore enhances man's mastery over nature—is the interpenetration of perception with *all* aspects of man's conceptual power. The totality of science—the highest form of human labor—assumes the dialectical unity between theory, practice, and purpose.* Theory suggests practice, which suggests social purpose, and natural and social practice induce further or better theory and vice-versa.

In the imperialist scheme, however: "The prevailing credo of contemporary social [and scientific] inquiry limits reason to an analysis of those means which will lead most effectively to given ends; reason is strictly precluded from passing judgment on the ends themselves . . ." [28] The intellectual is limited to "pure" inquiry disregarding even the question of social value. He is also less and less able to determine the nature of the problems he may wish to explore.[29]

Such limitations do not *yet* preclude the possibility of meaningful scientific work for the intellectual may still engage the naturalistic dimension of philosophy for scientific evaluation and unification. They do however engender an extraordinary degree of alienation.

Having lost control over the purposes of his investigative work, and increasingly unable to determine that which he wishes to investigate, the organic link between man's work and the self-conscious ends he sets for himself in his work is broken. The intellectual stands in an alien relationship to the product of his activity; and from the investigative process itself—"the act of producing."

To divorce means from ends, thought from action and fact from value is to divorce science from philosophy, perception from conception and man from himself. His research stands "outside himself, independently, alien, an autonomous power, opposed to him . . ." The inherently irrational char-

* Purpose could also be viewed as the *social aspect* of practice. In other words, there is practice in the naturalistic and social realms, corresponding to the philosophical division.

acter of imperialism collides with the inherently rational character of science, to such a point and in such a variety of ways, that reason itself becomes a menace to the imperialist order. We have the intensification of scientific inquiry on the one hand, and the eclipse of science on the other.

The limitations on reason eventually damage even the scientific purpose of science; and this, in turn, further aggravates the problem of alienation. For in order to limit reason to "pure" inquiry it is necessary to create the illusion that science is inherently neutral; whereas, of course, scientific laws in themselves have no social value. Their value is *socially determined;* and it is precisely for this reason that there is an *essential* (dialectical) unity between theory, practice and purpose through which we achieve the totality of science. This dialectic is operative *independent* of the scientist's will. Natural laws once discovered will be applied, and they assume their positive or negative social value depending upon the prevailing priorities of the social order. The social responsibility of the intellectual is not some additional tangential burden to be assumed by a few good samaritans. On the contrary, it is an essential, organic component of the scientific enterprise itself.

For in the era of the scientific-technological revolution when science is becoming a direct productive force, it has a *direct* social impact. Consequently, the philosophical function must *simultaneously* project both the scientific discovery and its immediate social dimension(s); it must *ascend* from the interpretive passivity of defining scientific and technical feasability to the active resolution of social problems. That is, the dialectic between the naturalistic and social dimensions of philosophy presents itself in a new way.

If it is possible to prevent disease, why not prevent it? If it is possible to end starvation, why not end it? If it is possible to wipe out illiteracy, why not eliminate it? If world war must be averted (within the context of sanity which is a constituent part of reason) then what must be done to avert it?

Scientific progress compels social revolution; and collaterally, the social revolution becomes the only reasonable (or sane) basis for the continuation of science. In this way science itself becomes a *motive force* for socialist revolution; and the essential elements of science, reason and life, likewise become a motive force for revolution. The scientific and social revolutions are simultaneous, causal and interpenetrating.

In the imperialist order it thus becomes essential to "neutralize" science lest it assume its revolutionary potential. To do this it is necessary to disengage the social aspect of man's conceptual power; that is philosophy must be "stabilized" so that science may be effectively "neutralized." But in the conscious and systematic effort to "stabilize" philosophy and "neutralize" science the dialectical unity between theory, practice and purpose is disrupted. Once that unity is damaged the whole enterprise is in jeopardy. The natural and social sciences are increasingly reduced to the intricate perfection of purely *technical skills*—descending to "ever more exquisite levels of absurdity." In the process of "stabilization" the social sciences are made into the exact antithesis of themselves; and the "neutralization" of science signals the beginning of the end of science itself. *For in the modern education industry the "stabilized" philosophy rests its theoretical laurels upon the denial of causality in nature.*

The denial of causality derives from a *philosophical* interpretation of quantum theory in physics which was most succinctly formulated by the German physicist Werner Heisenberg (1927):

> In the sharp formulation of the law of causality: "when we know the present with precision we can calculate the future" not

the conclusion is wrong, but the premise. On principle we *cannot* know the present in all its determining factors.* Therefore all perception is a selection from a multitude of possibilities and a limitation of future possibilities. Since the statistic character of the quantum theory is so closely linked to the inaccuracy of all perceptions, one might be led to the conclusion that behind the per-

* Following are two brief excerpts from different sources which give a relatively clear explanation of the scientific discovery from which Heisenberg's *uncertainty principle* is derived: "The crux of the problem is well known: For the scientist causality is that kind of regular connection between phenomena which makes it possible to calculate the future state of reality when its present state is known. Newton's classical mechanics was the most perfect expression of this traditional causality. According to Newton, the universe was composed of mass points, each of which has a definite position and a definite momentum. It was thought to be enough to measure the present positions and momenta in order to calculate the future positions and momenta and thus to predict . . . the future of the universe. Modern quantum mechanics however, showed that it is not possible to measure the present positions and momenta of microparticles, such as electrons, with equal precision. Smaller particles, such as neutrinos, are even destroyed when subjected to measurement. For to measure those particles we need light, which, according to Einstein, is composed of light quanta (photons). When we measure the electron's position it is struck by light quantum, so that its original momentum is altered by an uncontrollable amount. The shorter the wave length of the light used, the bigger will be the alteration in the electron's momentum, for the shorter the wave length, the bigger the light quanta. Unfortunately, light of shortest wave length is needed to measure with precision the electron's position. Thus, the more precise the measurement of the electron's position, the less accurate will be the measurement of its momentum, and vice-versa. This means that in principle the precise measurement of the electron's position and that of its momentum are mutually exclusive, so that we cannot know the present state of the universe . . ." [31]

To put it in another way: "Reducing the uncertainty in the position of the electron increases the uncertainty in the extent of the disturbance [of its momentum]; and reducing the uncertainty in the extent of the disturbance increases the uncertainty in position.

. . . There is no way to "see" the atom in operation; it does not matter whether the "observer" is a human being or a piece of equipment . . . Nor does it matter whether the observation was originally arranged by an intelligent and purposeful creature or is simply a whim of nature. Information about position always interferes with information about velocity. You can know one precisely, or you can know the other precisely, but you can never know both precisely together . . ." [32]

ceived, statistical world, a "real" world is hidden, which is governed by the law of causality. But such speculations seem to us sterile and meaningless—and we wish to emphasize this opinion. *Physics is only supposed to describe the connection of perceptions in a formal way.* The true situation can better be characterized in the following way: Since all experiments are subjected to the laws of quantum mechanics, *the invalidity of the law of causality is definitely proved by quantum mechanics.*[30]

The *uncertainty principle,* that is, that we cannot precisely and simultaneously measure the positions and momenta of microparticles, is a natural law. It is not the law but the *philosophical* interpretation of it that is in dispute. Heisenberg's conception of causality, "when we know the present with precision we can calculate the future" is the philosophical conception of the Newtonian Era. But that conception is not an eternal given, unless one believes it originates with Divine Authority. Rather than to abandon causality altogether, the problem is to develop the philosophical conception of it— a point we shall develop at some length momentarily.

Heisenberg, having denied causality, must and does proceed to assert the end of science itself—". . . physics is only supposed to describe the connection of *perceptions* in a formal way . . ." [emphasis added]. Heisenberg abandons the conceptual function *altogether.* Scientific inquiry is limited to purely quantitative analysis. Experiments, with an infinite variety of controls, may be performed and the details recorded. Such effort will undoubtedly yield valuable data; but unless that data is unified and evaluated it remains scientifically and therefore socially useless. Heisenberg explicitly reduces physics and much of science to technical labor and the scientist to technician and clerk.

Philosophy is made extraneous; for in the abandonment of all conceptual functions it is delimited to clarifying scientific concepts by means, for example, of logical and semantic analysis. Such is the philosophy of the modern logical positivists: "A kind of revolt of philosophers against philosophy, an antiphilosophical philosophy . . .";[33] that is a "stabilized" philosophy.

There is no longer anything to evaluate because evaluation depends upon causality. There is nothing to unify because unification presupposes theory, and the theoretical is likewise dependent upon causality. Philosophy itself is decimated:

> Whatever in contemporary philosophy is not irrelevant is still likely to be *remote* . . . There is . . . an unmistakable trend toward formalism and scholasticism. From a lively awareness of the problems of men we are moving to merely academic concerns, and these in turn are couched more and more often in the jargon of remote technicalities . . .[34]

With the invention and perfection of the "antiphilosophy" the illusion of a socially neutral science can be created and maintained. But by so emasculating the conceptual function it is increasingly difficult to evaluate and unify even in the purely naturalistic realm—a tendency in modern western science which is now accentuated to the point of crisis by the qualitatively new way in which the naturalistic and social dimensions of philosophy interpenetrate.

At a recent meeting of the American Association for the Advancement of Science (AAAS), for example, one scientist noted with alarm that U.S. universities are producing "surprisingly conservative hence uncreative scientists." He attributed this to the "academic pressure for positive results [making] research people disinclined to invest time and effort in more speculative thinking . . . [the university scientist] puts more value on publication per se, scooping the competition, satisfying his curiosity, or satisfying his boss than he does in producing results which will be useful to others in changing their view of nature . . ."[35]

Through all of this the natural sciences exhibit a profound

internal resilience for evaluation and unification of data in the naturalistic realm may continue and meaningful scientific inquiry may proceed for a time in various fields. Consequently, in the beginning, the agony of the natural scientist over his social responsibilities is generally posed as a moral *dilemma:* to produce and the social consequences be damned; or to cease production and the consequences be damned again; or it is posed as a universal dilemma in which somehow "the world" is itself responsible for all of its own ills. A distinguished biologist put the question this way:

> The ominous paradox of the modern world brings us together . . . All of us . . . students, scholars and scientists are joined by a powerful bond. We share the frightful task of seeking humane knowledge in a world which has, with cunning perversity, transformed the creative power which knowledge generates into an instrument of catastrophe.[36]

Posed in this way, however, the moral and political issues appear irresolvable.

Given the intrinsic qualities of science—its essential humanism and radicalism; and given the nature of the present systemic crisis, it should be increasingly apparent that the moral question to be confronted is, in actuality, the survival of science—indeed, the survival of reason—itself.

The behavioral and social sciences on the other hand, have little internal resistance to "stabilization" and are quickly left in shambles—a technical shell of their former selves, computing and modifying the behavioral and social patterns of "objectified" man. The tendency toward a nonevaluative posture in the social sciences—the preoccupation with technical and quantitative analysis—is also not new. Robert S. Lynd, in his classic study of the social sciences almost forty years ago, challenged this concept of objectivity:

> Nobody questions the indispensability of detachment in weigh-

ing and appraising one's data. But in other respects, as a matter of fact, current social science is neither as "neutral" nor as "pure" as it pretends to be . . .[37]

Lynd continued: "Research without an actively selective point of view becomes the ditty bag of an idiot, filled with bits of pebbles, straws, feathers and other random hoardings." [38] It is here in the social sciences, that the inhumanity and madness is first apparent, and the intellectuals' alienation is often most keenly felt.

For the direct social impact of science, most especially in the midst of the social chaos now characteristic of the society, *requires* that the organic unity between scientific and scholarly inquiry and its redeeming social value be consciously and simultaneously projected, else the intellectual will experience an extraordinary sense of *irrelevance, which is the alienation of labor in its most acute form.*

The ecstasy of technical perfection, the intrinsic epistemological joy of science, once stripped of its social value (or assuming a negative social value) is rendered a delusion. The intellectual descends into what Noam Chomsky describes as "a morass of insane rationality," and having lost control over the purposes of his work "is himself made worthless."

In the hands of the corporate controllers the social conditions of intellectual labor are the exact antithesis of what they ought to be: creativity is discouraged, if not penalized; reason crippled, if not scorned; humanism spurned, if not denied. Man is "objectified." Science is "neutralized." Philosophy is "stabilized."

And so it must be. For if both dimensions of reason are exercised, and all aspects of philosophy are operative, the essential radicalism and humanism of science will prevail; and its identity with social revolution in the present era will increasingly define its priorites and purposes.

7 MARXIST PHILOSOPHY

Heisenberg's philosophical interpretation of the *uncertainty principle* is the generally accepted theoretical premise (whether explicit or implicit) for the natural and social sciences in the United States.*

From Heisenberg's sharp formulation of the law of causality—when we know the present with precision we can calculate the future—he concludes that the laws of quantum mechanics definitely prove the invalidity of the law of causality. It is not Heisenberg's conclusion which is wrong, but his definitive premise which *uncritically embraces* the Newtonian concept of causality; namely, that of *mechanical determinism*.

Lenin, writing before the discovery of quantum mechanics, already presented challenges to the deterministic philosophy (as did Marx and Engels):

The really important epistemological question that divides the philosophical trends is not the degree of precision attained by our descriptions of causal connections, or whether these descriptions can be expressed in exact mathematical formulas, but whether the

---

* Operationalism, as developed by P. W. Bridgman (see Chapter IV), has its philosophical origins in Heisenberg's philosophical interpretation of the *uncertainty principle*.

source of our knowledge of these connections is objective natural law or properties of our mind, its innate faculty of apprehending certain *a priori* truths, and so forth. This is what irrevocably divides the materialists Feuerbach, Marx and Engels from the agnostics (Humeans) Avenarius and Mach . . .[1]

The philosophical system of mechanical determinism has two fundamental features: First, it projects cause and effect as rigidly opposite poles without any regard for their interaction; second, it assumes that an objective description is one which *necessarily* excludes the observer. The purpose is to discover how things are in their "real" state—that is, to "see" how they really are when they are not being observed.

In rightfully rejecting this deterministic conception of causality in nature, Western sciences simultaneously abandoned causality, and *replaced* it with the theory of probability; thereby, in *actuality* accepting the deterministic model of causality. Probability, however, is not a theoretical *substitution* for causality. Rather, it is a theoretical *development* of our conception of causality.

In this connection we may consider two aspects of probability—one methodological, the other theoretical. First, as a statistical method it allows us to predict probable effect (or the possibility of an event). Second, it modifies and extends our philosophical view of causality.

Causal laws are those which establish the *necessary* relationships between objects, events, conditions of other things at a given time and those at later times:

At this point, however, we meet a new problem. For the necessity of a causal law is never absolute. For example, let us consider the law that an object released in mid-air will fall. This in fact usually happens. But if the object is a piece of paper, and if "by chance" there is a strong breeze blowing, it may rise. Thus, we see that one must conceive of the law of nature as necessary only if one abstracts it from *contingencies,* representing essentially independent factors which may exist outside the scope of things that can be treated by the laws under consideration, and which does not follow necessarily from anything that may be specified under the context of these laws. Such contingencies lead to chance. Hence, we conceive of the necessity of a law of nature as *conditional,* since it applies only to the extent that the contingencies may be neglected . . . We see, then, that it is appropriate to speak about objectively valid laws of chance, which tell us about a side of nature that is not treated completely by the causal laws alone.[2]

The *uncertainty principle* allows us to develop our conception of causality to include the random fluctuations (the laws of chance) which are, in fact, an essential aspect of the normal functioning of many different things.

There is an additional consideration. We now know that any particular process or phenomenon is ultimately caused (and effected) by an *infinite* number of factors. At the same time, of course, we know that our knowledge is finite at any particular historical moment. Therefore, *we can never know everything there is to know about a particular phenomenon or process,* although we may deepen and broaden our comprehension of it.

We can however seek to determine which factors bear a *decisive* relationship to the phenomenon or process, and which factors bear only a *tangential* or *remote* relationship to it. That is, we can distinguish between those factors which *cause* a phenomenon or process, and those factors which may *affect* its causes. To make such a distinction meaningful a *dialectical* view of the relationship between cause and effect is essential (as opposed to the rigid separation characteristic of mechanical determinism). We can then conceive of the organic unity between causality and chance.

In addition to its denial of causality in nature, Western scholarship still generally accedes to the mechanical conception of objectivity. The "objectiveness" of a scholarly work is largely measured by the extent to which the scholar (observer) succeeds in absenting himself from its presentation and its conclusions. In the rigid application of objectivity, evaluative functions are emasculated and the social sciences are again thrust toward the technical computation of data, since evaluation and unification would necessarily invite the "subjective" views of the observer. From this premise it is only a short distance to the conclusion that *partisanship and objectivity must be mutually exclusive.* From there to the carefree niche of value-free social scientist (or "neutral" scientist) there is no distance at all.

The *philosophical* alternative to mechanical determinism is *dialectical materialism.* This is the vital significance of Lenin's conclusion that the theory of socialism "arises side by side with the class struggle and not one out of the other." The Marxist philosophy of dialectical materialism does not arise spontaneously; *nor does it arise as the self-serving justification for a social movement.* Classical Marxist philosophy grows out of a long and arduous struggle within the intelligentsia itself, to develop a philosophical system correspondent to the materialist conception of Nature; that is, a philosophy founded upon the *materialist* conception of history.

Through much of the eighteenth and nineteenth centuries natural scientists fought to break science away from philosophy, and with good historical justification: ". . . The philosophy of the Ancients and the schoolman was adapted to religion and politics and not to the material handling of Nature. It was a hindrance and not a help to science . . ." [3] While scientists sought this isolation from philosophy, they were nevertheless, under its domination, for it existed and exerted its influence independent of their will. Engels explained the problem this way:

Natural scientists believe that they free themselves from philosophy by ignoring it or abusing it. They cannot, however, make any headway without thought, and for thought they need thought determinations. But they take these categories unreflectingly from the common consciousness of so-called educated persons, which is dominated by the relics of long obsolete philosophies, or from the little bit of philosophy compulsorily listened to at the university (which is not only fragmentary, but also a medley of views of people belonging to the most varied and usually the worst schools), or from uncritical and unsystematic reading of philosophical readings of all kinds. Hence, they are no less in bondage to philosophy, but unfortunately in most cases to the worst philosophy, and those who abuse philosophy most are slaves to precisely the worst vulgarized relics of the worst philosophers.[4]

It is out of a struggle against the obsolete philosophies that Marxism emerges as the *philosophy of science:*

Marx has not elaborated a new philosophy unifying the world of knowledge and absorbing science, but he has rather added to the knowledge of humanity the instruments of science; in short, Marx's *dialectics do not regress science to philosophic reason, but introduce philosophic reason into scientific intellection.*[5] (emphasis added).

Marxism must also therefore, be a *scientific philosophy.* That is, in order to serve as the philosophy of science it must provide a *materialist* conception of history:

From this [materialist] point of view the final causes of all social changes and political revolutions are to be sought not in men's brains, not in men's better insights into eternal truth and justice, but in changes in the modes of production and exchange. They are to be sought, not in the *philosophy* but in the economics of each particular epoch.[6]

For Marx philosophy *ascends** to political economy. Marx confirms his view of man. Men are to be distinguished from other animals not by their consciousness, but by their ability to produce their means of subsistence. Correspondingly, and fundamental to *materialist* (as opposed to idealist)

---

* The German word *Aufhebung,* frequently used in Marxist writings, is a much better description of what we mean for it contains a dual meaning: philosophy not only rises to political economy, but it is also *uplifted,* enlightened, its perspective broadened by that process.

philosophy, consciousness is *determined* by social being, and not vice versa.

Philosophy as science is a *dynamic* body of knowledge. It is a *dialectical* system. " . . . Once an historic element has been brought into the world by other elements . . . it also reacts in its turn and may react on its environment and even on its own causes . . ." [7] In the Marxist system there is no longer a rigid separation of cause and effect, but a conceptual (dialectical) unity between them.

Further, Marxism provides for a dynamic unity between theory and practice. The Marxist philosophy is *animative*. It necessarily discards the static, contemplative and mechanical concept of objectivity which must, by its very posture, assume the functional stability of society. Marxism embraces *partisanship as an essential component of objectivity.* *"For Marxists the concrete analysis of the concrete situation* is not the opposite of 'pure' theory; on the contrary, it is *the culmination of all genuine theory,* its consummation, the point where it therefore breaks into practice." [8] By its very affinity with the materialist conception of nature, Marxism assumes that in the "real" state of affairs there is in fact, a natural and constant interaction between the observer and what he observes; and further that there is constant change which in the social sphere, may be evaluated relative to, partisan to one's definitive view of man as worker.

In its identity with change the Marxist philosophy is unique.

No longer does it position itself *inside* thought; no longer is it concerned with the idea of the nature of the world, while leaving it as it is, but with changing the world that engenders such illusions. In a profound sense, "the solution of theoretical enigmas is a task for praxis." [9]

From all of this Marx presents his challenge: "The philosophers have only *interpreted* the world in various ways; the point, however, is to *change* it!" This is the "Copernican

Revolution" in philosophy. "Marxism," wrote Antonio Gramsci, "is a philosophy which is politics, and a politics which is also philosophy."

Many students and intellectuals studying the causes of campus disorder have concluded that the breakdown of the university is not primarily political. One faculty commission studying the Berkeley campus of the University of California, for example, wrote: "The campus suffers from more than political ills and more than political prescriptions are required to cure its malaise . . . the fundamental problem of the campus is rooted in education . . ." [10]

The Commission is, of course, correct. The fundamental problem is rooted in education; but the educational crisis is *profoundly political* because at the heart of that educational crisis lies a philosophical system predicated upon the denial of causality in nature and the emasculation of conceptual and evaluative functions.

The maintenance of that philosophical posture becomes a *political necessity* for the imperialist elite; just as it is abundantly clear what the alternative philosophical system would do to politics!

8 NOTES ON THE REBELLION

The spontaneous response of students and professors to the general crisis of the society, and the general intellectual-educational crisis of the university has been as confused, varied, inspired, penetrating and astonishing as any other revolt by people suddenly become a part of the working class. Many observers have been stunned by the fury and intensity of the demonstrations. Protests have been sustained and vigorous, sometimes attaining extraordinary peaks of passion and enjoying the support of tens of thousands of young people.

While particular issues remain at the core of each protest, much more than that is involved. Experiences during the Free Speech Movement at Berkeley illustrate this point. That controversy began in mid-September 1964. Students were told by the university administration that they could not organize political activity, or advocate off-campus social action, on university property. That was the issue. The students saw a clear and defensible principle; that is, that constitutional rights exercised off the campus, such as advocacy and political organizing, had to be equally exercisable on the campus, free from administrative restraint and subject only to the jurisdiction of the courts.

The protest against the new regulations began with students setting up "illegal" tables on the campus laden with literature advocating off-campus political and social activity. Early in October campus police sought to arrest a former graduate student who was manning a table for the Congress of Racial Equality (CORE). They brought a police car onto the campus' main plaza and placed the arrested man in it. As they attempted to leave several hundred students spontaneously sat down around the car, preventing its departure. For some thirty-six hours hundreds of students remained seated around the car.

At 6 P.M. the following day more than 900 police were assembled on the campus. Leaders of the demonstration were negotiating with the administration. If there was no settlement by 7 P.M. the police had orders to break up the sit-down. Thousands now gathered around the car in a spontaneous burst of sympathy for their fellow-students. In staccato speech, they told each other what to do if the police moved in: remove your earrings; loosen your ties; take off pins and watches, etc.

The vast majority had never been in a demonstration before, much less been faced with a police onslaught and the real possibility of arrest. Most were terrified. Many wept openly. You would suggest that they leave; that there were enough people to maintain the protest; but most would refuse. The police were finally withdrawn from the campus just before 7 P.M. when a temporary agreement between the students and the administration was reached. The crisis had, for the moment, subsided.

There was a principled issue at the core of that demonstration, but more than a single principle was needed to evoke such a display of courage. There was a shared, if not yet articulated sentiment that the authority of the university it-self had to be challenged; that many things about it were wrong; that the world stood on its head; that everything was upside down and inside out; and that somehow, some-body, everybody had to straighten it out before we all died for no plausible reason—just as we all seemed to be living for no plausible purpose. There is no other way to explain the presence of that quaking, still joyful, mass of people, clinging to each other.

This general (even unarticulated) distress, disaffection, disillusion of the students and professors is a reflection of the fact that the imperialist social order is in general and acute crisis. The society is moribund. Its very existence becomes antithetical to life. Again, events on the Berkeley campus are apropos.

Early in 1969 faculty and students from the department of environmental design, in conjunction with some Berkeley residents (many of them students) living just south of the campus, conceived of and built a park on an empty, appar-ently forgotten lot. They planted grass and trees and flowers and small shrubs; they built a playhouse, swings and a sand-box for children. This people's park soon began to perform a vital social service for young mothers who left their children in the care of other students in order to attend classes, or go to the library, etc. Most important of all, the park was aestheti-cally pleasing. It was actually *pretty*.

The Regents of the University soon disclosed that they owned the vacant lot and intended to convert it into a park-ing lot and ball field. The Regents were adamant; the stu-dents were appalled, then outraged.

In the awful battle that followed police shot and killed one young man, blinded another, and shot more than 110 other people (most of them in the back, according to hospital reports). Hundreds were arrested; scores were beaten; the entire campus was bombed with tear gas (the CS variety) dropped from a low-flying helicopter. The National Guard occupied a two-mile area around the campus for a week; and police were actually photographed gleefully ripping up newly planted shrubs and flowers. All of this happened so that the Regents could build a parking lot! Surely this is a civilization gone mad.

A university in the midst of such madness must shed any illusion of social neutrality; it must become an instrument for progressive social change or it too becomes antithetical to life, and therefore the antithesis of itself. As the university becomes a constituent part of the production process (and therefore an instrument for the practical consolidation of the system) the illusion of the university's social neutrality *is* increasingly exposed. Therefore, from those who accept the status quo and deliver apologies for the university's "inevitable" role we often get misanthropic theory and cynicism. If on the other hand there is resistance to the status quo, to the use of university as an instrument of oppression, we get the development of a radical consciousness. But, in the spontaneous burgeoning of this consciousness there appear many different and apparently contradictory forms of resistance; and likewise many confused, apparently contradictory ideas about the source of the crisis and how it is to be resolved. However (and this is the most important aspect), the spontaneous revolts, whatever their limitations, revealed to the Marxist movement, a new quality of social reality in advanced capitalist society, and exposed the basic contradictions of the system, and its fundamental inhumanity, in a refreshing and unique manner.

The intellectual's alienation, while rooted in the same material conditions as the manual worker, differs in the particular because of the specific characteristics of mental labor, and because the intellectual, while becoming a constitutent part of the working class, does not find himself at the *point* of production. The change in the class position of the intellectuals is not primarily caused by themselves physically moving from the superstructure of society to its economic base; rather, it is caused by the movement of the superstructure itself which interpenetrates with the base in a qualitatively new way. In other works, the changed position of the intellectuals is primarily a consequence of the socialization of the production process as a whole. Correspondingly, the spontaneous rebellion of the intellectuals and the evolution of their consciousness differs from that of the industrial working class.

The intellectuals, still attached to the superstructure of the society tended to see first its social injustices; and their protests tended to center on issues such as racial oppression and the war in Vietnam. The inability of the social order to resolve these crises—and in fact the official resistance to their resolution—forced many intellectuals to reevaluate their previous assumptions about the system itself.

The tenacity of the government in defending the war, and the persistent duplicity with which it reported its actions and policies created a "credibility gap" of chasmal proportions. It became increasingly apparent that the war in Vietnam could no longer be explained in terms of an "unreasonable aberration" from a basically sound foreign policy. Somehow it must be related to a system which the Marxists call "imperialism."

It is at this juncture that many of the academic activists concluded that injustice might in fact *characterize* the social order; that domestic oppression and international intervention might somehow be organic to (or an inherent part of) advanced capitalist society; that some form of radical change, some mechanism for "revolution" might be "activated" to set things right.

The intellectuals passionately and spontaneously embrace the slogans for revolution *before* they develop any theoretical or scientific conclusions as to the *nature* of revolution. They come to their radical awakening from a *structuralist* view of the society, in which they cannot, by dint of their own experiences perceive the basic exploitative features of the system. Until they develop class consciousness* their conception of revolution is *idealist* rather than *materialist,* utopian rather than scientific.

Furthermore, given ". . . the growing irrationality of the capitalist system, intellectuals increasingly transcend it in thought and arrive at socialist convictions . . . " But unless their new consciousness embraces a recognition of the class struggle ". . . it easily gets lost in its own idealist abstractions. This expresses itself in an intellectualized view of the struggle as existing *solely* in the realm of consciousness." [1]

The spontaneous revolts of the intellectuals, even their planned strikes reflect these limitations. There is the frequent fetishism of revolutionary "purity"; issues are posed in absolute moral terms; there is a lack of political practicality; and a disdain for organization.

Their conception of imperialism is, on the whole, a structuralist one in which the *internal* contradictions of imperialism—as the highest and last stage of capitalism—are not easily envisioned except in terms of the national and racial oppression of Black and Brown peoples. The intellectuals develop an anti-imperialist consciousness devoid of class consciousness. Their sole affinity is with the movements for national liberation at home and abroad. They do not generally conceive of the national liberation movements as an

---

* We note that manual workers also do not *spontaneously* develop class consciousness, but that the discipline and experiences of work at the point of production make them less susceptible to the particular fetishisms of the intelligentsia.

essential component of the class struggle in the era of the disintegration of imperialism.

Additionally most intellectuals come to their anti-imperialist conclusions at the same time that they retain many notions of chauvinism and elitism inherited from their position and function. Thus, many will embrace the revolutionary slogans and even the goals of the Black and Brown liberation movements, and *at the same time,* ignore the daily manifestations of racism in their own universities and in their own scholarship (not to mention the daily atrocities committed in nearby ghetto communities and by the society in general).

While the primary contradiction affecting the intellectuals is rooted in their new relationship to the production process, the sharpest struggles on the campus have tended to be social rather than economic ones. There is not a one-to-one correlation between the primary contradiction and the sharpest point of struggle, and there need not be. However, as social conditions of work within the university tend to assume more and more of the characteristics of an industry, the faculty and students spontaneously begin to seek out the traditional forms of struggle developed by the workingman: they organize trade unions.

As might be expected, faculty trade unionism assumes its own peculiar traits; but a union is a union and the trustees know it, even as the professors may at times try to obscure it in the aesopian language of their profession. The sectors of the education industry first affected by trade unionism are those most directly and immediately affected by industrialization —the state and junior colleges. The sixties marked a definite nationwide surge in union membership among college faculty, and the trend was clearly discernible in California.

In 1962 there were 5,056 college teachers in the California Federation of Teachers (CFT); in October 1969 there were 11,722. The union's growth, of course, reflects the general increase in the number of teachers. There are three other significant factors to be considered in evaluating the union's growth. First, between 1960 and 1969 there was not only an increase in total membership, but the spreading of the union into previously unorganized institutions, from the state colleges to the junior colleges and the University of California. Second, the movement toward union organization is strongest among the younger and usually more vulnerable professors. In a number of instances union locals were begun but their young organizers were "not rehired" for the next academic year or denied tenure and the fledgling locals could not survive. Third, early in 1970 the CFT in the state colleges merged with the Association of California State College Professors. The new independent faculty organization is united around five general areas of concern: obtaining adequate salaries; improving educational quality and controlling the increase in workloads for each professor; obtaining professionally acceptable promotion and sabbatical leave provisions; resisting efforts to centralize power in the state colleges; and countering the threat to eliminate the right to tenure.

On the whole the California Federation of Teachers represents a small proportion of college teachers in the state; and nationally too, only a small percentage of the college faculties are organized. Still, the trend is unmistakable. By 1971 the largest *professional* organization of university professors, The American Association of University Professors (AAUP) was actively seeking collective bargaining rights on behalf of professors in a half dozen different states.[2] The Wayne State AAUP chapter (in Detroit) filed a petition on February 12, 1971, with the Michigan Employment Relations Commission for certification as the faculty's collective bargaining representative. Similar activity has been undertaken by AAUP at Eastern Michigan University, Oakland University,

Michigan State University, and the University of Detroit, reflecting the accelerated AAUP interest in collective bargaining in Michigan.

Similarly, AAUP chapters at Fordham University, Adelphi University, New York University, Manhattan College, Columbia University, St. John's University, and elsewhere in New York are seeking collective bargaining arrangements with their respective boards of trustees. There are comparable developments in leading universities in California, Connecticut, and Pennsylvania.

Even among students there have been fleeting attempts to organize unions—such as the Free Student Union at the Berkeley campus which in the few months of its existence in 1965 enjoyed a membership of some 3,600 students. An economics professor, writing in the *New Republic* in November, 1970, predicted that student activism would continue even if the war in Vietnam was ended; and he proposed collective bargaining methods as a way of settling student–administration disputes. He even proposed legislation to legalize student strikes, and prevent student expulsions for such activity.[3]

The initial response of other students and professors (*not excluding those organized into unions*) to their changed status, may be an attack "not against the bourgeois *conditions* of production, but against the instruments of production themselves . . ."[4] One of the earliest reflections of this, and one still widespread in the rebel camp, is the creation of "free universities" or "experimental" programs, some of which have had a tendency to become therapeutic rather than educational centers, *abandoning the rigors of science in the mistaken belief that its discipline is the source of their alienation.* These programs may descend into various forms of religiosity and mysticism; or they may replace the creativity of the disciplined scholar with aimless speculation. A more sophisticated attack on science may come from the "super"-radical perspective. Here there is an insistence that science is inherently or essentially a bourgeois phenomenon *in itself,* and must be destroyed if the "revolution" is to be secured. This rhetoric is now sometimes accompanied by the physical destruction of university facilities. In either case the abandonment of science creates only the illusion of resistance.

As the radical movement among students and professors matures it begins to focus more of its attention on the actual social conditions within the university itself, and on the structure and control of the institution. In this way the revolt moves from abstract social issues to the concrete realities of university life and the concrete relationships of power within the university; then, this experience, in turn, deepens and concretizes the intellectuals' view of the social issues, and the general crisis of the society.

Within the Left movement on the campuses, a two sided but interrelated struggle unfolds. There is an analytical-theoretical struggle and a tactical-strategic one. How can all the social and economic crises be brought together into a coherent political theory? Should they be unified into one theory? What should be the political strategy of the movement? Are we for reforms or do they serve solely as vehicles of cooptation? Are we for "confrontation politics"? Are we for or against violence? and so forth.

Within the university itself there is a two-sided educational crisis manifested in the irrelevance of course material on the one hand; and the "insane rationality" of crippled analysis on the other. There emerges then a four-dimensional struggle within the university as a whole. For the two-sided educational crisis interpenetrates with the theoretical/analytical and tactical/strategic struggle within the Left movement, often producing the apparently incomprehensible behavorial patterns of the rebels, and the crazy-quilt pattern of spasmodic revolt.

Consider the following: An historian with a brilliant and essentially radical analysis of U.S. history has conservative, even reactionary political views, hating the students in general and the radical students in particular, more than he detests the trustees who run his college. Or the professor, say, in sociology, with radical political positions on most significant social issues who cannot integrate his political views into his academic discipline. There is a seemingly incomprehensible separation between his politics and his scholarship in which he accepts the basic theoretical premises of bourgeois sociology at the same time that he is a member of his local teachers union and leads an anti-war protest. Or a student who considers his education to be irrelevant and abandons all serious study of social and scientific problems to become a "full-time revolutionary." The more fervent his abuse of science and scholarship, to paraphrase Engels, the more he may become a slave of the worst vulgarized relics of the worst bourgeois theorists and philosophers; and the more he may tend to embrace anarchistic and terroristic tactics in his frenzied assault against "the system."

The intellectuals' attraction to anarchist philosophy and anarchist tactics also forms a contradictory pattern. On a tactical level, radical students are easily attracted to disruptive actions—and for good reason. Away from the point of production they are unable to grind the economic machinery to a halt. When students go out on strike (and they have, of course) the university continues to function unless that strike precipitates a political crisis, or enjoys faculty support and ultimately the support of the organized trade union movement. Events on the Berkeley campus offer a vivid illustration of this.

Navy recruiters came to the campus in November, 1966, and set up shop in the student union. The students promptly organized a picket line around it. They also asked a community organization—Women's Strike for Peace—to set up its table next to the Navy recruiters. They did; and the administration sent in several campus police officers who confiscated the peace table. Students sat down around the Navy table and the confrontation was on. Scores of city police were called to the campus and skirmishes between students and police continued for several hours. The next morning leaflets called for a student strike to protest the whole affair, and in particular the presence of police on the campus.

The students responded and picket lines soon sprang up everywhere. Thousands got involved, even many who had not been on the campus the day before. Noon rallies were attended by anywhere from 5,000 to 10,000 people (depending on the weather). People actually picketed for hours in the pouring rain. The teaching assistants' union, AFT Local 1570, voted to join the students' strike. They had many of their own grievances to settle as well as their general sympathy for the student walk-out. The administration finally agreed to begin "discussions."

Meanwhile the campus, by-and-large, continued to function; and the strike dragged on for days, with final examinations approaching. In fact it became apparent that while many students were attending the noon rallies and voting to continue to strike, they were at the same time attending classes! The AFT chapter sought strike sanction from the local AFL-CIO Central Labor Council. The Council indicated that it would grant strike sanction if the administration took any disciplinary action against the teachers. The administration announced that it would not take any such action, at that time (later, it did). Strike sanction was denied, and the strike ended. It was not so much a defeat as it was a stalemate.

The strike officially ended with two mass meetings—one for the teachers, the other for the students. Each meeting voted to end the walk-out and then concluded its business with a song. The students sang, "We All Live in a Yellow Submarine," and the teachers sang "Solidarity Forever." The symbolic meaning of that moment was unmistakable. Among radical students the concept of "confrontation politics," physical disruption and even destruction, the general thrust toward anarchist tactics took hold and emerged as a dominant trend. Growing out of the same frustration an explicitly apolitical, "cultural" revolt emerged as well. However, and this is of decisive consequence: the *mass* of students —most of whom were vehemently opposed to the war, racial oppression, and poverty, and frustrated by their own "irrelevant" studies—nevertheless decisively rejected both tactical lines. Many adopted the dress and cultural posture of the rebel movement, though even here the identification tended to be temporary and superficial.

At the same time this same mass of students was deeply attracted to anarchism philosophically. At a moment when many of them for the first time perceived the crushing authority of the university (and, by extension, the state), and experienced a loss of individuality and a depersonalization, anarchist philosophy with its uncompromising rejection of the state, and its emphasis on the supremacy of the individual became very appealing indeed. Still, this philosophical attraction to anarchism did not materialize into an anarchist movement among the mass of students. In fact, the anarchist tactics of the radicals isolated them from their fellows, and by the spring of 1970 during the Cambodian crisis the massive campus upheavals were led (where they had any leadership at all) by generally independent students, often described as "moderates"—a term which did not refer to their philosophical or ideological views, but to their tactical approach.

The same general experience that attracts students and professors to anarchism also attracts them to Marxism. The clearest and most consistent trend among the intelligentsia has, in fact, been the continuing and growing interest in Marxism, the working class and socialism. This is true in terms of what people are reading, and more important in terms of what they are studying and writing about.

Lenin's description of the spontaneous revolts of the workers in the Russia of the late nineteenth century bears a striking resemblance to the spontaneous revolts of the intelligentsia in the United States sixty years later:

. . . The spontaneous element, in essence, represents nothing more than consciousness in *embryonic form*. Even the primitive revolts expressed the awakening of consciousness to a certain extent. *The workers were losing their age-long faith in the permanence of the system which oppressed them and began—shall I say not to understand, but to sense the necessity for collective resistance,* definitely abandoning their slavish submission to the authorities. But this was nevertheless, *more in the nature of outbursts of desperation and vengeance than of struggle* . . . the workers were not, and could not be conscious of the irreconcilable antagonism of their interests to the whole of the modern political and social system, i.e., theirs was not yet Social-Democratic [Marxist] consciousness. In this sense, the strikes * . . . still remained a purely spontaneous movement . . . We have said that there could not have been Social-Democratic consciousness among the workers. It would have to be brought to them from without . . .[5] [Emphasis added.—B.A.]

Lenin's theory of the limitation of spontaneity, and his conclusion that the workers could not spontaneously develop a socialist revolutionary consciousness, *is just as valid for the modern intelligentsia.*

This is all the more true because with the emergence of the radical movement there is a concerted effort by certain

* Lenin is referring to widespread strikes in Russia during the 1890's.

sections o fthe bourgeoisie (especially the Liberal wing of it) to restrict and divert the theoretical and political development of the rebels; or to co-opt them into the established political structure; or if that is unsuccessful to contain them within ineffectual enclaves of mysticism and eroticism.

The intellectuals *as a whole* cannot and will not spontaneously develop a socialist revolutionary consciousness. It must be brought to them, just as it must be brought to all the constitutent sections of the working class. And, of course, only a portion of the intelligentsia, as only a portion of the working class as a whole, will join the revolutionary party itself, though a great majority may eventually identify themselves with the goals of the revolution and consciously embrace it.

The point is not what consciousness starts to do on its own. For ". . . out of all such muck we get only the inference that three moments, the force of production, the state of society, and consciousness [have] come into contradiction with one another . . ." [6]

The modern socialist theory, the Marxist philosophy can now be introduced into the *social and scientific struggles* of the intelligentsia as a whole, where for the first time the *social conditions within the university allow that to be done.*

9 PROBLEMS OF ACADEMIC FREEDOM

The politicalization of the American university is one of the most striking features of the decade. Yet traditionally most intellectuals have taken a dim view of politics. The concerns of the true scholar were to transcend the petty considerations of political partisanship. The institutional integrity of the university lay precisely in its ability to rise above the material considerations of political intrigue which led inevitably to compromise and corruption.

In the academic mind the conception of politics is narrow and restricted: "In America politics means bargaining and compromise between organized groups for limited and usually material prizes . . ." [1] Political struggle is identified with opportunism and expediency to the virtual exclusion of principle. Political activity, it is argued, " . . . contaminates the search for truth and jeopardizes academic freedom. Politics means partisanship and partisanship is the enemy of truth . . ." [2]

The aversion to the political world is a recurring theme in the literature on higher education. It underlies the conception of the ideal university as an independent and neutral entity: ". . . if the universities are to render any service toward the right solution of social problems of the future," states the 1915 *Declaration of Principles* of the American Association of University Professors (AAUP), "it is the first essential that the scholars who carry on the work of the universities shall not be in a position of dependence upon the favor of any social class or group, that the disinterestedness and impartiality of their inquiries and their conclusions shall be, so far as humanly possible, beyond the reach of suspicion." [3]

Apprehension of the political world lies at the core of much of the contemporary student and faculty concern over the increasing politicalization of the campuses. The politicized university, however, is primarily a consequence of the new functions the university must assume as a constituent part of the productive process, and as an essential instrument for the practical political, economic, and ideological consolidation of the system. The university, *as an institution,* has become a *direct* productive and social force. It has thus lost its institutional neutrality to an unprecedented degree in the present period.

This has precipitated a profound crisis in defining or redefining the principles of academic freedom.[4] For these principles, as they were developed in the United States at the end of the last century and the beginning of this one, were based upon the assumption that institutional neutrality was the prerequisite of intellectual freedom.

According to these principles:

Academic freedom consists in the absence of, or protection from, such restraints or pressures—chiefly in the form of sanctions threatened by state or church authorities or by the authorities, faculties, or students of colleges and universities, but occasionally also by other power groups in society—as are designed to create in the minds of academic scholars (teachers, research workers, and students in colleges and universities) fears and anxieties that may inhibit them from freely studying and investigating whatever they are interested in, and from freely discussing, teaching, or publishing whatever opinions they have reached.[5]

The abolition of restraint holds with this exception: *the obligation of the intellectual to employ the scientific method in his deliberations.* The 1915 AAUP *Declaration* affirms that:

> The claim to freedom . . . is made in the interest of the integrity and progress of scientific inquiry; it is therefore, only those who carry on their work in the temper of the scientific inquirer who may justly assert this claim. The liberty of the scholar within the university to set forth his conclusions, be they what they may, is conditioned by their being conclusions gained by a scholar's method and held in a scholar's spirit; that is to say, they must be the fruits of competent and patient and sincere inquiry, and they should be set forth with dignity, courtesy, and temperateness of language.[6]

The traditional view of academic freedom also embraces the principle of self-government; that is, the right of the faculties to govern themselves in determining all scientific and scholarly matters, including their exclusive right to evauate each other's work and qualifications:

> It is, however, . . . inadmissible that the power of determining when departures from the requirements of the scientific spirit and method have occurred, should be vested in bodies not composed of members of the academic profession. Such bodies necessarily lack full competency to judge those requirements; their intervention can never be exempt from suspicion that it is dictated by other motives than zeal for the integrity of science; and it is in any case unsuitable to the dignity of a great profession that the initial responsibility for the maintenance of its professional standards should not be in the hands of its own members.[7]

The German concept of academic freedom, embodied in the principles of *Lernfreiheit* and *Lehrfreiheit,* influenced the American view to a considerable extent. *Lernfreiheit* meant that German students were free to determine what courses they wished to take and in what sequence. They did not have to attend their classes regularly and they were exempt from all tests except the final examinations. They lived in private residences, and controlled their own lives. *Lehrfreiheit* referred to the freedom of the professor to investigate anything he wished and to report his findings in lectures or in published form. He enjoyed freedom of teaching and research.[8]

The Americans, however, did not adopt all aspects of the German view. For example, they neglected the concept of *Lernfreiheit*—the academic rights of the students. The 1915 AAUP *Declaration* begins: "It need scarcely be pointed out that the freedom which is the subject of this report is that of the teacher. . . ." [9]

Further, in the United States academic freedom included the freedom of "extra-mural utterances and action," while the German view distinguished between freedom *within* the university and freedom *outside* the university. Within the walls of the German university, ". . . a wide latitude of utterance was allowed, even expected. . . . But outside the university, the same degree of freedom was not condoned . . . it was generally assumed that professors as civil servants were bound to be circumspect and loyal, and that participation in partisan politics spoiled the habits of scholarship. . . ." [10]

The educated members of the eighteenth and nineteenth century European and American society were, in their overwhelming majority, from the propertied classes; and if one owned property it was generally assumed that one would not pose a serious threat to the established order. Thus, the propertied classes tended to enjoy greater freedom traditionally and in law, than the bulk of the population. This further assured the greater degree of academic freedom permitted students and scholars within the university. Moreover, well into the eighteenth century a person accused of a crime could "Plead Clergy"—which meant that he could read and write—thus to demonstrate his class origins and escape with a lesser penalty as established *by law*.

The American view of academic freedom bears a definite similarity to its view of political liberty: in its tendency to emphasize the absence of restraint; in its assertion of self-government; in its elitist assumptions. Of course there is a philosophical correlation. But academic freedom should not be viewed as the extension of the Bill of Rights to the campuses. Academic freedom is something quite distinct. In the European tradition, for example, it "antedates general freedom of speech by several hundred years, and its development was quite separate and independent." [11]

In the United States the earliest assertions of academic freedom in the eighteenth century and the first half of the nineteenth century were not shaped by any consistent principles. There was ". . . a tendency on the part of the institutions to defend themselves from outside attack and to assert their right to stand for unpopular causes . . . [which] stemmed in part from the colleges' function as preserver of ancient traditions. . . ." [12]

The modern concept of academic freedom was developed in the United States in the aftermath of its Civil War, and in the wake of the Darwinian revolution in science. At this juncture science was able to advance a ". . . special conception of truth and a formula for tolerating error that had the effect of investing academic freedom with an ethic." [13] The primary function of academic freedom then, is to protect the integrity of science and scholarship, and to provide for the uninhibited progress of scientific and scholarly research. Academic freedom exists independent of the Constitution, although it does not have the force of law and does not contravene the constitutional rights applicable to all citizens.

The most important *philosophical* distinction between constitutional freedoms and academic freedom is that while the constitution guarantees the *absolute* absence of re-straint—"Congress shall make *no* law abridging freedom of speech. . . ."—academic freedom does not. The claim to academic freedom is conditional—it assumes the scholar's obligation to engage in scientific and scholarly study.

This essential feature of academic freedom was to a large extent abandoned by sections of the liberal intelligentsia in its efforts to protect itself from the Rightist assaults upon academic freedom in the late nineteen forties and early fifties. While the 1915 AAUP *Declaration* was acknowledged, its content was often obscured. A new interpretation of academic freedom—as the *absolute* freedom of teaching and research based upon the freedoms guaranteed by the Bill of Rights as elaborated by the courts [14]—emerged as an important theme in the early fifties and persists today. This absolutist thrust is a serious distortion of academic freedom. Moreover, it does not confront the Rightist challenge at its point of attack.

When Professor Sidney Hook of the Philosophy Department of New York University attacked the right of members of the Communist Party to teach he was not primarily challenging their rights of free association under the Constitution. Rather, he asserted the incompatibility of Communist Party membership with scientific and scholarly work: "No present member of the Communist Party can honestly fulfill his vocation or his unspoken commitment as a scholar and teacher to the ethics and logic of objective and scientific inquiry." [15] When the Board of Regents of the University of California sought to fire the Communist philosopher Angela Davis, they used the Hook thesis in their presentations. The issues in the *Davis* case, and in all similar cases, cannot be joined by defending the inviolability of the individual's rights under the Constitution. The issues are joined by establishing the substance of the Communist view, the purpose of Marxism, and the objectivity of its methodology. Here the defense of academic freedom depends upon the demonstration of *at least* the compatibility of Marxism with science. Only at that point does the Rightist view sustain a fatal blow.

The absolutist defense of academic freedom is a serious distortion; and the absolutist concept now presents a grave danger to scientific and scholarly work as we shall try to illustrate. The 1915 AAUP *Declaration* has serious limitations, but it does remain as a definitive statement of the purpose of academic freedom.

The restrictions assumed in the exercise of academic freedom do not inhibit the natural and social sciences. On the contrary such restrictions are essential to their further progress:

> There is no doubt that the advance of science benefits humanity, excepting of course, the development of weapons of mass destruction. But it is not so clear that scientific research demands an absolute freedom of speech and debate. Rather the evidence suggests that certain kinds of unfreedom place no obstacle in the way of science, while other kinds may indeed completely stifle fruitful investigation . . . Despite restrictions, which in the case of religion are taken as the very stigmata of an unfree society, science flourishes and human happiness is advanced. . . .[16]

For example, would anyone, in the name of academic freedom seriously propose that the Physics Department of the Massachusetts Institute of Technology retain a member of the Flat Earth Society to teach its students that the earth was flat? Or, would anyone propose that the Biology Department at Harvard retain a professor to teach its students that Darwin's *Origin of Species* and the *Book of Genesis* were equally acceptable explanations for the origin of man? Of course not; and one need not be a Marxist to affirm that, though the principle is exactly in accord with a central aspect of the Marxist concept of freedom. As Lenin expressed it: "Those who are really convinced that they have made progress in science would not demand freedom for the new views to continue side by side with the old, but the substitution of the new views for the old." [17]

Yet the example of Darwin's *Origin of Species* competing with the *Book of Genesis* is not imagined. The former State Superintendent of Public Instruction in California, Dr. Max Rafferty, proposed such a program, and the Board of Education voted its approval. It was expected to be instituted in all public elementary and secondary schools in California until the voters defeated Rafferty in the 1970 elections. Still, the program was to have been implemented in the name of academic freedom! The Rafferty Plan demonstrates a critical fact: the Rightist assault on academic freedom is not primarily directed against the Constitution. *It is a calculated assault upon science as a feature of its effort to maintain the status quo.*

The world of Fundamentalist delusion notwithstanding, the effort to develop the concept of academic freedom so as to protect science, without simultaneously subjecting it to abuse, is a difficult theoretical and practical problem. For once the element of the absolute is rejected, the freedom of the individual scholar, or a group of scholars, to present their views depends upon their method of investigation and the substance of their findings, and the relationship of those two factors to the general state of science, and the general political atmosphere. Such considerations are clearly fallible and may subject the individuals, and science, to considerable abuse, a fact of which every partisan of socialism is painfully aware.

However, the alternative method of absolute freedom in the academic realm is even more unacceptable. For it reduces science to nothingness. The earth could be flat or round; man could have evolved or be the creation of God, and so forth. The theory of absolute freedom has to assume the *a priori* invalidity of all discovery; deny the possibility of discovery; and therefore reject the concept of progress altogether. It is, in fact, the theoretical and practical correlative to Heisenberg's philosophical interpretation of the quantum theory which, by assuming the invalidity of the law of causality in nature, also assumes the *impossibility* of discovery.

In affirming the desirability of restraint we are, of course, cognizant that its implementation can cut both ways. That is, the same *method* of argument used by the Left against the CIA can be used by the Right against Communists. But there is no reasonable alternative to this. The issues cannot be joined by arguing for the absence or exercise of restraint. The point is to establish the nature and purpose of scientific and scholarly work.

In maintaining this position we are accepting the distinguishing feature of the 1915 AAUP *Declaration*. However, we can no longer identify institutional neutrality with academic freedom. On the contrary, the concept of neutrality is becoming increasingly destructive of it. There is, of course, an aspect of scholarly neutrality that is not to be discarded. It is the method of investigation. While any scientist or scholar begins his work with a definite point of view, the method of his investigation is objective. That is, his conclusions are the result of thorough, nonsectarian and nondogmatic investigation, research, observation, experimentation and critical analysis. His conclusions are not the *a priori* resolution of a problem (after which he gathers only that evidence which he knows will support a prior conclusion). But in many academic minds neutrality has come to mean something else; namely, a devotion to tolerance and moderation as virtues in themselves.

A widespread assumption in the academy, for example, is that intolerance is symptomatic of irrationality; or to put it another way, that tolerance is a function of reason. This view corresponds to the pluralist conception of society in which tolerance is viewed as the pre-eminent virtue of a pluralist democracy. Still, in itself, torn from a social context, tolerance is a function of nothing. In particular circumstances it is a function of irrationality.

For example, the *Harvard Educational Review* (Winter, 1969) published an article by Arthur Jensen, a prominent educational psychologist, entitled: "How Much Can We Boost IQ and Scholastic Achievement?" Jensen concludes that there are significant *genetic* differences in the intellectual IQ capacity between racial groups, especially Blacks and whites; that is, he concludes that whites are genetically superior. The article inspired major controversy. Many scholars wrote lengthy and damning refutations. A few rebuked Jensen for "scholarly irresponsibility." [18] Another professor reported approvingly, by way of contrast, that: ". . . a very distinguished American scholar displayed what I take to be an authentically tolerant reaction to Jensen. When asked whether he thought Jensen was a racist or not, the scholar replied 'what does it matter?' There was a time when such a response in the academy would have been taken for granted . . . " [19]

It need scarcely be pointed out that racism is demonstrably unscientific. The *scientific* refutation of it is overwhelming Racist theory is as obsolete as the pre-Copernican notion that the earth is the center of the universe. Racism is a totally irrational bias which will, at frequent intervals, prevent the investigator from reasoned, objective, and critical analysis. A racist is not a scholar, much less a scientist. This is above all true in the United States with its history of racial oppression affecting every dimension of life, every aspect of the society. Tolerance of racism is a manifestation of profound irrationality.

This view has now been confirmed for all practical purposes by the National Academy of Sciences. At its meeting in Washington, D.C., in October, 1971, the Academy refused to authorize a study, proposed by William Shockley of Stanford

University, to further investigate the alleged hereditary differences between Black people and white people affecting variations in intelligence ratings. Shockley had presented a paper to the Academy in 1968 in which his conclusions were virtually identical to Jensen's thesis. Shockley's major conclusion was that the alleged lesser intellectual performance of Black people was genetically determined. The October, 1971, action of the National Academy of Sciences certainly inhibits the "freedom" of Shockley and others to engage in such research. Clearly, however, this inhibition advances the cause of science and therefore of academic freedom.

In the academic mind neutrality has also come to mean the absence of partisanship. Partisanship, it is argued, breeds passion, and while passions may be noble they are seldom rational; hence, they blind the scholar to critical and objective judgment; they diminish his analytical capabilities. The idea that passion is antithetical to reason; or to put it another way, that moderation is a function of reason, is, as one social psychologist observed:

an underlying assumption widely accepted in the Western world among social scientists and among the general public . . . [All] moderately liberal and conservative ideas are deemed equally "healthy," while outside the fold of conventional moderation, it is assumed, cool rationality has given way to neurosis or at least unreasoning passion.[20]

Yet moderation and passion, in themselves, are a function of nothing. The question always is: to what end?

The dogmatic assertion of neutrality becomes, finally, Kafkaesque. In May, 1970, a professor of physics at the Berkeley campus of the University of California, Charles Schwartz, was disciplined by the Chancellor for "exceeding his authority as an instructor" and violating the academic freedom of his students. Professor Schwartz had required those students who wished to enroll in his course to take a "Hippocratic Oath" which read: "The purpose of science should be the general enhancement of life and not causing harm to man. I affirm that I will uphold this principle, in teaching and in practice, to the best of my ability and judgment."

A section of the Berkeley faculty supported the Chancellor's decision to reprimand Professor Schwartz. Yet the logic of this position is appalling. For it follows that it would be a violation of academic freedom to restrain a bacteriologist from developing more virulent strains of bubonic plague for use in airborne attacks. It follows too, that it would be a violation of academic freedom to prevent a medical researcher from injecting human "specimens" with cancerous cells. The "neutral" scientist, "liberated" from all restraint, thus finds that it is irrelevant to evaluate the social purpose of scientific and scholarly work altogether, and that to make such an evaluation or to affirm a humanist partisanship might constitute a violation of academic freedom! The insistence upon neutrality and the absence of restraint in the face of such realities is, quite literally, madness. Indeed, the heart of imperialism is irrationalism, ". . . the eclipse of reason, the denial of science, the repudiation of causation. The normal result is cynicism; the abnormal is sadism. The finale is fascism . . ." [21]

The allusion to fascism is not rhetorical. Research in chemical and biological weaponry is presently being conducted in the United States. In the context of the absolutist view of academic freedom there is no way to stop such efforts. Consider, then, by way of logical extension our present inability to prohibit medical research on human "guinea pigs," which of course happened in Nazi Germany. Dr. Andrew C. Ivy, who aided the prosecution at Nuremberg, has written of this unbelievable medical degeneration:

. . . I believe it is important for the medical profession to be aware that this Nazi infamy was not merely the infamy of a few crazed, psychologically twisted practitioners. It appears that fewer than two hundred German physicians participated directly in the medical war crimes; however, it is clear that several hundred more were aware of what was going on. Now it appears evident to me that this "witches' sabbath" of medical crimes was only the *logical end result of the mythology of racial inequality and of the gradual but finally complete encroachment on the ethics and freedom of medicine by the Nazis* when they were in the process of gaining control of the German government. And this process, so far as I know, went unopposed by the German medical profession . . .[22]

The "experiments" conducted by the Nazi doctors included testing people's tolerance of high altitudes (subjection to low pressure), exposure to low temperatures and the drinking of sea water. There were other hideous experiments with typhus and infectious jaundice; experiments with sulfonamide, bone-grafting cellulitis, and mustard gas; euthanasia; and experimental work in mass sterilization. It has been concluded from all of the evidence, that the Nazi doctors who tortured concentration camp prisoners to death in their experimental laboratories produced not a single new cure, nor did a single important medical discovery result from their experiments.

Essential of our discussion of academic freedom is the fact that the university has lost its institutional neutrality. Hence, our point of departure is different. We assume that institutional partisanship already exists. Our problem then, is: what is the nature of that partisanship; what is its impact upon the substance and methodology of intellectual labor; is it destructive of the academic enterprise or does it contribute toward the further development of scientific and scholarly work?

This is the point of controversy on dozens of campuses. When students and professors demonstrate for the abolition of ROTC are they violating the academic freedom of the students who may wish to enroll in that program and the officers who wish to teach it? When students and professors demand that counter-insurgency research be banned from a campus are they violating the academic freedom of the behavioral scientist? When students and professors demand that a project in chemical warfare be terminated are they violating the academic freedom of the chemist? Is the demand that the university sever its relations with the CIA a violation of the academic freedom of the political scientists who may wish to work on such a project?

A distinguished historian offered this defense for denying the CIA access to the university:

> . . . the CIA is, by definition, subversive of the academy. Its business is subversion at home and abroad. . . . It has by its own admission, subverted universities, scholars, student organizations, research, publications, even churches and philanthropic institutions. Its whole character is at war with what the university stands for. It loves secrecy, but the university flourishes only in the light. It takes refuge in anonymity, but the university must know the credentials of those to whom it gives its confidence. It is chauvinistic, but the university is by its nature cosmopolitan and international. It works not to find and certainly not to proclaim truth, but the major purpose of the university is to extend the frontiers of truth. . . . Whatever we may think about the larger place of the CIA in the scheme of national defense, we can scarcely avoid the conclusion that it is degrading for the university to lend its facilities, and . . . reputation . . . to cooperate in its own subversion. It is degrading for it to extend the hand of fellowship to those who are engaged in perverting its character.[23]

This is exactly the point. There is no violation of academic freedom in demanding the termination of CIA-sponsored projects, ROTC Programs, CBW research and the like. On the contrary, if the partisanship which now prevails demands that the university serve as an instrument for the practical consolidation of imperialism, as we believe it does; and if the inherent irrationalism of imperialism conflicts with the essential rationalism, humanism and radicalism of science and scholarship as we have sought to demonstrate throughout this book; *then the defense of academic freedom requires opposition to such partisanship.*

10 THE RADICAL RECONSTRUCTION OF HIGHER LEARNING

In accepting a basic premise of the traditional view of academic freedom—that is, that it exists to insure the integrity of science and scholarship, and that the exercise of restraint in this connection is necessary and desirable—it follows that the concept of academic freedom, in an era when the university has become a direct productive and social force, *must be developed in order to preserve its essential features.*

Academic freedom is no longer a function of institutional neutrality. Instead it has become a function of the partisan evaluation of teaching and research; of the dynamic assertion of humanist principles; of the conscious projection of an anti-imperialist partisanship and a revolutionary perspective. That is, the integrity and progress of scientific and scholarly work now requires the *reconstitution* of the university in all its spheres: altering the content, purpose, scope, and form of the educational process; providing new criteria for admission to the university; projecting a new perspective for the relationship of the university to the community; establishing new priorities for research and development; and challenging the ideological functions of the university in both theory and practice. Ultimately it will mean the reconstitution of political power in the governance of the university.

The struggle to reconstitute the university, then, is an integral part of the whole revolutionary process. It is not a demand; nor is it a tactical device. It is a strategic concept. It represents, if you will, the class struggle of the intelligentsia as a whole in advanced industrial-imperialist society; and it therefore embraces both the scientific and social struggles of the intelligentsia.

The thrust toward reconstitution has already begun. The most significant efforts have been made by Black, Chicano, Asian and Native American students (and professors). This is another manifestation of the continuous interaction between the academic rebellion and the liberation movements, especially the Black movement. Many of the recent proposals for Ethnic Studies represent the essence of reconstitution in that they redefine the relationship of the university to the community.

The proposals for a Third World College presented in February, 1969, by the Third World Liberation Front (TWLF) at the Berkeley campus of the University of California are a case in point. The TWLF prospectus for the Third World College began with this statement of purpose:

The Third World College will focus on contemporary problems of urban and rural living of Third World peoples. Therefore, its primary goal is to produce students having knowledge, expertise, understanding, commitment and desire to identify and present solutions to problems in their respective communities.

Thus, the mission of the Third World College is to focus on contemporary living and produce scholars to address the problems and issues that accompany it.

In this respect the Third World College will be significantly more community-oriented and community-based than is the case with other academic structures to be found on this campus.[1]

The TWLF then presented a sketch of the overall structure

of the Third World College designed to encourage the greatest possible interaction between the Black community and the College:

The College of Third World Studies as currently proposed will be part of the Berkeley campus of the University of California and will house and coordinate several new departments, institutes, and programs focused on the history, culture and contemporary life of some important Third World groups in the United States which have been traditionally left out of the main stream of education at this university. In addition, the College of Ethnic Studies will also house the new Institute on Race and Community Relations which has already been approved on this campus, and the Third World College extension programs.

The department will focus on offering courses and curricula of formal academic studies. The Institute will not engage directly in regular course instruction but would specialize in other activities including research, community service, publications, leadership training, and fellowship programs. These activities would be consistent and coordinated with the academic programs in the departments. The Institute would contain within it centers with a special focus on each ethnic group. Thus, an Afro-American Center, a Chicano Center should be part of this Institute. They will address themselves to the needs of the particular Third World community. There will be a high level of community participation in the work of the Institute.

The new College of Third World Studies will bring together under one administration the Institute, the previously mentioned departments, the extension division, and other programs yet to be developed that will focus specifically and deliberately on community-oriented programs of instruction, research, cultural and community development.[2]

In providing for the administration of the College the TWLF sought to insure that the dean of the College, and the faculty and staff responsible for implementing and developing its proposals, would be technically appointed by the University's chancellor, but only with the advice and consent of the Third World students and faculty. Additionally, again reflecting its community orientation, the staff of the College was to include not only students and professors, but members of the community who would share responsibility for the development of curriculum, and other college programs.

Further, the criteria for admission to the Third World College was altered to take into consideration the particular experiences of Ethnic peoples in the United States:

> Students will be admitted directly into the College of TW Studies as freshmen or transfer students ready to declare as a major one of the fields of study within the college and graduate students working toward an advanced major.
>
> . . . the College will admit older community members who have not finished high school and who have distinguished themselves in practical experience in the community. . . .
>
> . . . In admitting students to this College consideration will be given not only to the standard university admissions criteria but to other factors as well, including ethnic related cultural experiences and the participation in the community and the general level of ability and talent.[3]

The specific course material proposed for each of the Ethnic Studies Programs demonstrated the seriousness of the effort, and more importantly, the infinite variety of subjects now open to investigation. The Black Studies Program,[4] for example, established new areas of inquiry such as African Philosophy; the Black Writer in America; Comparative Black Anthropology. It proposed courses usually neglected in the larger university: Introduction to Afro-American Art; History of Black America; Black Thought in the Twentieth Century; Survey of Afro-American Literature. It offered courses designed as explicit alternatives to dominant trends in U.S. scholarship: Sociology and the Black Family; Psychology and Racism; Racism, Colonialism, and Apartheid; Humanism in Perspective. Finally it offered courses to deal with specific problems in the Black community: Black Americans and the Third World (politics of liberation); Police in the Black community; Survey of Education (from elementary to college level); Current Economic Problems of Afro-Americans; the Economics of Racism; Black Social and Political Welfare.

The official opposition to the TWLF proposals was substantial. For nine months administrative authorities buried them in the labyrinth of "official channels." When the Third World students finally struck the Berkeley campus to secure the implementation of their program, the full fury of the State's military and police power was unleashed against them. Leaders of the TWLF were arrested a dozen times each; some were beaten unconscious on the main plaza of the University in full view of students and professors. The chancellor's office counseled patience, and maintained that the TWLF was being unreasonable in its demands and in its insistence that its proposals were "non-negotiable." The Berkeley faculty voted to support the concept of Ethnic Studies, but equivocated in supporting a College devoted solely to Third World affairs. The majority of white students were sympathetic to the proposals but most remains politically aloof from the strike. A union of teaching and research assistants (American Federation of Teachers, Local #1570) joined the strike. After six bitter and bloody weeks it ended, the issues largely unresolved. The University muddled on its way with a series of compromises and accommodations primarily designed to "keep the peace."

While the TWLF strike, and dozens of efforts like it, have suffered momentary set-backs, their significance transcends their immediate tactical goals. For the concept of the Third World College projects the strategic direction for the radical-democratic and revolutionary movements.

The key to reconstitution lies in the dynamic it seeks to create between the college and the community. Reconstitution redefines the relationship of the university to society, and in this way transforms the university itself. No longer is the university to serve as the preserver of tradition in monastic seclusion. No longer is it to serve as the political, philosophical, and practical instrument for the maintenance of the status quo in an ivy-shrouded sanctuary. The university is to become an instrument for progressive social change, and therefore an integral part of the community it is to serve.

Third World College
University of California, Berkeley

Black Studies Program

—Proposed Courses—

Anthropology
1. Introduction to Black Anthropology (Physical)
2. Cultural Anthropology
   a. Survey to African Anthropology
   b. Survey to Afro-American Anthropology
3. Upper Division
   Comparative Black Anthropology

Dramatic Arts
1. Afro-Americans and the Theater
2. Workshop (improvisation)

Economics
1. Economics of Racism
2. Current Economic Problems of Afro-Americans

English
1. Survey of Afro-American Literature
2. Introduction to Black Prose and Poetry
3. The Black Writer in America
   a. Historical
   b. Theoretical

Art
1. Survey of African Art
2. Introduction to Afro-American Art
3. Survey of Contemporary Afro-American Art
4. Introduction to Revolutionary Black Art

Criminology
1. Social Control and the Black Community
2. Police in the Black Community

Education
1. Education (Knowledge) of the Black Man
2. Survey of Education from Elementary to College Level
3. Seminar—Upper Division

History
1. Black America
2. U.S. History from Black Perspective

Humanities
1. Humanism in Perspective

Linguistics
1. Ghetto Language
2. Survey of Black Dialect

Philosophy
1. Black Thought in the Twentieth Century
2. Introduction to African Philosophy

Political Science
1. Political Problems of Black Americans
2. The American Government—Black Perspective
3. Racism, Colonialism and Apartheid
4. Black Americans and Third World (politics of liberation)

Music
1. Music and the Black Man
2. Contemporary Afro-American Music
    a. Religion and Blues
    b. Jazz
    c. Rhythm and Blues
    d. New Musics

Psychology
1. Psychology of Racism
2. Black Economical and Social Psychology

Social Welfare
1. Black Social and Political Welfare

Sociology
1. Sociology and the Black Family
2. Black Social Movements
3. Black Social Institutions
4. Urbanization of Black People
5. Organization of the Black Community

In the reconstitution of the university the classical disciplines are not abandoned. On the contrary, reconstitution requires a full comprehension of the whole heritage of culture and knowledge. We do not dismiss Shakespeare or Aristotle or Diderot. Their relevance is universal and unending. But if taught in a social void and made antiseptic by purely technical dissection they *appear* irrelevant. If taken simply to satisfy some general education requirement they *appear* meaningless. As one professor posed it:

> . . . [J]ust what it means to have "had" Dostoevsky or Freud or Marx is, of course, problematical. It may mean that the student has read works by the author, brooded over the ideas and grown through his struggle to understand them. It may also mean that he has been intellectually immunized by being inoculated with small, weakened dosages of the author . . . [after which] he is assumed to be generally educated.[5]

The point of reconstitution is the revitalization of the traditional disciplines by placing the classics both in their historic context, and in a contemporary social milieu. In this way the discipline is socially useful providing the student with its particular methods and concepts and insights through which he may visulaize the problems of society—or any aspect of society—in a new and more interesting way.

Opponents of reconstitution maintain that ". . . a university that exists only as a service station for either the status quo or the revolution has ceased to be a place where people can think freely, where critical rationality can exist at all . . . ."[6] The concept of the university as a "service station" is an unhappy analogy because it does not define the actual relationship of the university to the society, and as a result proponents of this view are obliged to equate the status quo with the revolution. For example, when a car is serviced—supplied with certain necessities, or repaired—it does not interact with the service station, in that neither the intrinsic qualities of the car, nor those of the station are affected by the encounter. However, the relationship of the university to the status quo—i.e., to the social order—is quite different. The university interacts with the society. The intrinsic qualities of the university are directly affected, even to a large extent defined, by the nature of the relationships it assumes; and in turn the university directly affects the quality of the social order.

The university today is not a "service station"; rather, it serves the interests of the status quo. Either it maintains that posture, or it assumes a different one; that is, it serves as an instrument of progressive and radical social change. There is no escape from partisanship: "You are either part of the problem, or part of the solution." The real question is: what happens to the quality of the university if it serves as an instrument of radical change?

The proposals of the Third World Liberation Front did not lower the standards of scholarship; they redefined the purpose of scientific and scholarly work. They did not abandon the concept of objective and critical analysis; they strengthened both by redefining the concept of objectivity. (At times the regental attacks reached such a level of vituperation that one suspected that in the regental mind, if you were Black, you were by definition, incapable of objectivity!) The proposals did not abolish the traditional disciplines; on the contrary, they injected them with new life. By redefining the relationship between the university and the community the organic unity between scientific and scholarly work and its redeeming social value was forged in a new and vibrant way.

The unity between the campus and the community must be consciously projected. This is the practical corollary to the emergence of science as a direct productive and social force. If the philosophical function of the intellectual is, *in practice,* to ascend from the interpretive passivity of defining scientific and technical feasibility to the active resolution of social problems, then the relationship of the intellectual to the community must likewise ascend from the elitist assumptions of bourgeois political theory to the egalitarian principles of socialist humanism. The assertion of those principles need not wait for the revolution; indeed the struggle for their realization is part of the revolutionary process itself.

The reconstitution of the university must reflect the economic, scientific, technological, social, political, cultural, and aesthetic needs and aspirations of the working people at each particular moment, and in each particular community. The intellectual will have to confront the problems of automation, racial oppression, urbanization, exploitation, police violence, environmental pollution, the oppression of women, public transportation, public health, unemployment and so forth, *with* the community, at their point of impact; *with* the worker, at the point of production. At the same time the reconstitution of the university should reflect the economic, scientific, technological, social, cultural, political and aesthetic aspirations and needs of the intellectual by reestablishing the organic link between his scientific and scholarly work and its redeeming social value.

The convergence of interests between the intellectuals and the community is not continuous, and need not be. In fact, the tendency toward convergence may be accompanied by a divergence of interests due to the tendencies toward theoretical abstraction inherent in intellectual work, vital aesthetic considerations and the dynamic of the investigative process itself at times yielding unpredictable discovery and unexpected insight.

Still, in the main, the needs and aspirations of the working people will tend to define the aspirations and needs of the intellectual, *and vice-versa;* that is, the aspirations and needs of the intellectual will also tend to define the needs and aspirations of the people. The university experiences a true renaissance. Through this continuous interaction, the concept of reconstitution is constantly being transformed. It is always *becoming.* It develops and changes as the revolutionary process itself matures.[7]

In a tactical way the academic rebels have already acted to reconstitute the university. This can be seen, for example, in the "reconstitution" of classes during the Cambodian crisis in May, 1970, stemming from a moral imperative that normal routines could not continue while the U.S. government escalated the war and students were shot and killed at home. It can also be seen in the formation of organizations like Scientists and Engineers for Social and Political Action (SESPA) with members on many campuses, and in industry. Its slogan is "Science for the People." Among social scientists there are the formation of groups like Concerned Asian Scholars, and radical caucuses within the professional associations.

The idea of reconstitution is seen in the proliferation of Marxist and radical scholarly journals, many designed as specific alternatives to the official publications of the established professional associations such as: *Social Theory and Practice,* "an interdisciplinary and international journal of social philosophy"; *Yale Review of Law and Social Action,* "devoted to exploring methods for effecting social change"; and *Telos,* "committed to investigating new philosophical horizons that seek to rescue philosophy from the trivality and meaninglessness in which it presently finds itself." Likewise, it can be seen in the growth of radical research institutes such as the Pacific Studies Center near Stanford University; the Bay Area Institute in San Francisco; the North American Congress on Latin America in New York.

Similarly reconstitution is reflected in the statement of principles of the new faculty group, United Professors of California (UPC), which has as one of its objectives: "To promote efforts of educational institutions to secure funds and to secure political support for action on social, ethnic and economic needs in the adjacent communities as well as in society at large." The idea is also seen in the Eighty-Fourth Annual Convention of the Modern Languages Association (MLA) which adopted a "sense of the body" resolution calling for bi-lingual Chicano studies program [8]; and in the formation of the New University Conference (NUC), a coalition of radical graduate students and professors whose purpose is to organize "educational workers at their work place," and to develop a working-class consciousness among academicians.

Still, many of these new formations do not yet flow from a clear strategic perspective, and many retain an elitist view of society. To that extent they lose much of their political potential. Yet even as a tactical innovation reconstitution has encountered furious opposition. Reconstitution, as a national strategy, consciously projected as an organic component of the revolutionary process, will face even greater resistance. However, the strategy contains within it the resources to survive precisely because it alters the relationship between the university and the community.

The present tactical dilemma of the student movement comes from its political isolation. That isolation does not stem from the militant tactics of the students, their fascination with rhetorical imagery, or even the flirtation with terrorism. These are symptomatic of the isolation, and the consequent feelings of political impotence. However, the isolation of the student movement is primarily a reflection of the *real separa·tion* of the university from the community which actually exists in bourgeois society. The movement's preoccupation with tactical solutions to what is fundamentally a political problem is a major source of its diffusion and frustration.

The ability of the campus movement to obtain community support and sustain it now emerges in a new way. For with a strategy of reconstitution the intellectual need no longer plead for support with the vagueness of abstract virtue, utopian scheme or moral argument. He is now *of* the community. The unity is *real* arising from the politics of the struggle itself.

The intellectual is not an "ally of the working class" in the sense that he joins the struggle of the workers at the point of production by walking the strikers' picketline because he understands the objective need for alliance. Likewise, the worker is not called upon to support student demands for an end to ROTC programs or war research because he understands that his objective needs correspond to those of the students. Such a conception of the alliance between intellectuals and workers is mechanical and artificial. It is imposed upon both. It depends upon abstract consciousness for success, rather than the life experiences and actual needs of both. It does not reflect in practice what is true in theory; namely, that the scientific and social revolutions are now simultaneous, causal and interpenetrating.

With the ascendancy of science to a direct productive force the material conditions are created within the imperialist order in which the students, and social scientists, scientists and engineers—the intellectuals as a whole—will begin to become conscious that they are a part of the working class. Consequently their relationship to the revolutionary movement is transformed.

Historically, as we observed earlier, Marxists have considered the intelligentsia to be a constituent part of the bourgeoisie. On this basis the classical Marxist view held that only individual members of the bourgeois intelligentsia would join the revolutionary movement.

With the intelligentsia now emerging as an integral part of the working class this conception of the relationship of intellectuals-as-individuals to the revolutionary struggle is clearly inadequate. In the era of the scientific and technological revolution the intellectuals *objectively* emerge as an integral part of the revolutionary *process*. This happens independent of anyone's will. Today, therefore, while individual intelligentsia may ally themselves with counter-revolution (members of the political science department of Michigan State University, for example, played a vital role in consolidating the U.S. position in Southeast Asia), the ability of massive numbers of students and intellectuals to precipitate a nation-wide political crisis was clearly shown during the events surrounding the Cambodian invasion in May, 1970. A central question for the revolutionary movement is to what extent it can move the intellectuals to *consciously* become part of the revolution. We have sought to demonstrate that given the class shift taking place today it is possible to win hitherto unprecedented numbers of intellectuals and students actively to the side of the revolution.

Further, unless these spontaneous upheavals are organized; and unless we precisely define and consciously project this movement's relationship to the revolutionary transformation of society (and therefore its relationship to the proletariat and the Black and Brown liberation movements which constitute the core of the revolutionary movement) it will shatter into a thousand pieces.

Moreover, unless the Marxist intelligentsia and the revolutionary movement engage in the scientific and social struggles now unfolding, the intellectuals will remain, in their overwhelming majority, ideologically and politically tied to the bourgeoisie (just as other sections of the working class remain ideologically tied to the bourgeoisie in the absence of such struggle). However, in the era of the scientific and technological revolution, it should be clear that given the social functions of the intellectuals, tens of thousands of them must consciously emerge as a part of the organized resistance in practice if the socialist revolution itself is to succeed. This means that the struggle for the radical reconstitution of the higher educational system is not to be construed as a therapeutic device for alienated students. On the contrary, the struggle is vital to the maturation of the revolutionary forces.

In this context the Marxist intelligentsia assumes a particularly critical position. For the struggle to reconstitute the university requires discipline, collective action and, above all, organization. The campuses must not be abandoned by radical and Marxist scholars. The millions of students of the present and the future cannot be left to the mercies of the philistine scoundrels masquerading as scholars. Science and scholarship, the whole cultural heritage of the people cannot be left to the ravages of imperialism.

The relationship between the intelligentsia as a whole and the working people is not paternalistic. Nor does the intellectual stand apart from the worker. On the contrary, his own liberation depends upon the outcome of the class struggle:

. . . the emancipation of society from private property, etc., from servitude, is expressed in its political form as the *emancipation of workers,* not as though it is only a question of their emancipation but because in their emancipation is contained universal human emancipation. It is contained in their emancipation because the whole of human servitude is involved in the relation of worker to production, and all relations of servitude are only modifications and consequences of the worker's relation to production.[9]

The servitude of the intellectual is a consequence of the intrinsic qualities of the imperialist social order. It is, as we have tried to show, a modification of the worker's relation to production; that is, a consequence of the private appropriation of socially-produced wealth.

Thus the alienation of the intellectual is derived from the irrationality and inhumanity which defines imperialist society. Propelled by the logic of his work and the meaning of his life the intellectual must embrace a revolutionary perspective if he is to overcome alienation. The radical reconstruction of the university reestablishes the essential connection between the intellectual enterprise and its redeeming social value; it recreates the organic link between the intellectual's work and the conscious ends he sets for himself in his work. A philosophy professor put it this way:

. . . The problem for modern man—for all of us—is what to do with his life, how to create satisfying meanings beyond his place in a merely biological scheme of things and beyond the impoverished offerings of the commercial complex, how to break out of the suffocating circle of a preprogrammed social fiction. Education is criticism, vision, discovery. In a dying society, education at its finest *is* revolution . . .[10]

The socialist revolution at its finest is vision, discovery, liberation. It is the affirmation of life; the triumph of reason.

REFERENCE NOTES

1 THE CRISIS IN HIGHER LEARNING

1. Frederick Engels, *Anti-Duhring, Herr Eugen Duhring's Revolution in Science,* Foreign Languages Publishing House, Moscow, 1959, at 28–29.

2. Caleb Foote, *et al., The Culture of the University: Governance and Education,* Jossey-Bass, Inc., San Francisco, 1968, at 12.

3. *The New York Times Magazine,* Sunday, January 7, 1968, at 18.

4. Cited by Herbert Aptheker, "Alienation and the American Social Order," in Herbert Aptheker, editor *Marxism and Alienation,* Humanities Press, New York, 1965, at 20.

5. Frederick Engels, *Socialism—Utopian and Scientific,* International Publishers, New York, 1935, at 58–59.

6. Caleb Foote, *et al., supra* note 2 at 13.

7. Upton Sinclair, *The Goose-Step, A Study of American Education,* published by the Author, Pasadena, California, 1922, at 18.

8. V. I. Lenin, *On Youth,* Progress Publishers, Moscow, 1967, at 108.

9. *Ibid.*

10. V. I. Lenin, *What Is To Be Done?,* International Publishers, New York, 1969, at 32. (Originally published in 1902.)

11. *Ibid.*

12. Karl Kautsky, "On The Draft Programs of The Austrian Social-Democratic Party," *Neue Zeit,* 1901–02, xx. I, No. 3, p. 79; cited by V. I. Lenin, *What Is To Be Done,* at 40.

2   THE CORPORATE CONTROL OF HIGHER EDUCATION

1. Thorstein Veblen, *The Higher Learning in America,* A memorandum on the Conduct of Universities by Business Men, Hill & Wang, New York, 1967 (orig. 1918); Ferdinand Lundberg, *America's 80 Families,* Vanguard Press, New York, 1937; Hubert Park Beck, *Men Who Control Our Universities,* The Economic and Social Composition of the Governing Boards of Thirty Leading American Universities, King's Crown Press, New York, 1947.

2. Ferdinand Lundberg, *supra,* note 1 at 375–377.

School	Managing Group & Principal Donors	Endowment
	(1937)	
Harvard University	J. P. Morgan management. Largest donor: Standard Oil (Whitney, Harkness, Rockefeller)	$129,000,000
Yale University	Morgan-Rockefeller joint management, Largest donor: Standard Oil	$95,838,560
Columbia University	National City Bank management. Largest donors: Baker, Dodge, Gould	$69,576,915
Univ. of Chicago	Rockefeller management and principal donation	$65,389,498
Massachusetts Institute of Technology	DuPont management. Eastman, DuPont donors	$33,000,000
Stanford University	Southern Pacific Railway and California public-utilities management. Leland Stanford donor	$32,000,238
Cornell University	Rockefeller management. Various wealthy donors	$30,311,743
Princeton University	National City Bank management. Taylor, Pyne, McCormick, Dodge, donors	$26,929,810
University of California	Crocker, Giannini, Fleischacker, Doheny donors and management	$20,228,414
California Institute of Technology	Mellon management. Carnegie donation	$16,369,382

3. *See,* for example, William Barry Furlong, "The Guardsmen's View of The Tragedy at Kent State," *The New York Times Magazine,* June 21, 1970, p. 12. Contrary to popular expectations a fair proportion of the men in the National Guard unit responsible for the shooting at Kent State, were themselves full or part-time students, or recent graduates. Some had even attended Kent State a year or two before.

4. A revealing study of the opinions of 5,000 college and university trustees in the United States was recently made by Rodney T. Hartnett, *College and University Trustees: Their Backgrounds, Roles and Educational Attitudes,* Educational Testing Service, Princeton, New Jersey, 1969, 71 pp. Hartnett concluded that the "trustees do not read—indeed, generally never even heard of—the more relevant . . . books and journals [on higher education] . . . The Trustees generally favor a hierarchical system in which decisions are made at the top and passed 'down' . . ." For example, a majority believe campus speakers should be screened; 40 percent believe that the administration should control the contents of student newspapers; 53 percent believe it is reasonable to require loyalty oaths from faculty members; 92 percent believe that attendance at college is a privilege not a right; and 64 percent believe that the trustees and not the faculty should make tenure decisions.

5. Caleb Foote, *et al., The Culture of The University: Governance and Education,* Report of the Study Commission on University Governance, published by The Daily Californian, 1968, at 25.

6. Seymour M. Hersh, *Chemical & Biological Warfare,* America's Hidden Arsenal, Doubleday, Anchor Books, New York, 1969, at 223.

7. Jess Unruh Report, *The Challenge of Achievement,* A Report on Public and Private Higher Education in California to the Joint Committee on Higher Education of the California Legislature, 1969 at 21.

8. *Bulletin* of the American Association of University Professors, Autumn, 1971, Volume LVII, at 400 and 405.

9. In 1901, for example, Thomas Elmer Will, fired from his post as President of Kansas State College enumerated more than a dozen cases of summary dismissals of professors by university trustees. He accused them of firing scholars who supported the Populist Movement, held anti-monopoly views, attacked the enterprise of a nascent imperialism or were otherwise critical of the social order. *See,* Walter P. Metzger, *Academic Freedom in the Age of the University,* Columbia University Press, New York, 1955, especially pp. 139–193.

3   THE REVOLUTION IN SCIENCE AND TECHNOLOGY

1. John Kenneth Galbraith, *The New Industrial State,* Signet Books, 1967, at 377.

2. Lewis Mumford, *Technics and Civilization,* A Harbinger Book, Harcourt, Brace and World, New York, 1962, at 215.

3. Karl Marx, *Capital.* Volume I. International Publishers, New York, 1967, at 386.

4. Roger Garaudy, "Problems of the Revolution in the Developed Capitalist Countries," *Nuestra Bandera* [theoretical organ of the Communist Party of Spain] December, 1968/January, 1969, at 2.

5. Karl Marx, *supra* note 3 at 486.

6. Roger Garaudy, *supra* note 4 at 2.

7. This visualization of the electronic revolution is suggested by Jack Kurzweil, "Cybernetics and Society," January, 1970 [an unpublished paper]. It is also developed at considerable length in the book by S. Handel, *The Electronic Revolution,* Penguin Books, London, 1967.

8. Norbert Wiener, *The Human Use of Human Beings, Cybernetics and Society,* Discus Books published by Avon Books, 1967, at 23, 24–25, 27.

9. The comparative essence of this electronic revolution is conceived in similar terms by J. D. Bernal, *Science in History,* Hawthorn Books, Inc. New York, 1965 (originally published in 1954) at 558–559; ". . . it is not so much in the components themselves but in their connections that the real novelty of modern electronic devices resides. Again, for the purposes of war, it was necessary to make devices which could add and compute as rapidly as was needed to carry out the complicated operations of direction and rangefinding and the computation of shell and rocket trajectories. These made it possible towards the end of the war to develop the first fully electronic computing machines. As computing machines they started where the mechanical computing machine left off more than a hundred years before, when Babbage had attempted, at enormous cost, to set up a machine to calculate mathematical tables more quickly and more accurately than human computers could do. At the moment we are only beginning to sense the possibilities of electronic computation. Here we have a generalized means for translating into movement of electrons the complicated and orderly processes that are carried out in the computer's mind.

Such a machine can not only carry out precisely orders given to it, but it can—and this is the essential novelty—react to the unforeseen situations dependent on the value of the first stages of its own calculation. Like the servo-machinisms, of which it is a highly specialized and refined type, it can react to contingencies, and even already begins, in selecting concordant and rejecting discordant results, to show some of the characteristics of judgment and of learning, in finding out easier ways of doing things that have been done once and so to a certain extent making up its own rules as it goes along. In all this it must carry within itself a large number of data or bits of information, some provided from outside, others generated by the operation of the'machine and requiring to be held for further use, held indefinitely but releasable at call. This is the memory, the essential feature of electronic computing. While a certain number of memories are of a static kind, recorded by magnetic marks on tape or wire, or by assemblies of wires and magnetic loops, others depend on recycling the message indefinitely round an electronic circuit. Wiener has shown in his book that *cybernetics* (or steersmanship) is a new branch of creative science, linking mathematics, electronics, and communications engineering. It is guided by information theory and has links with the physiology of the nervous system and with psychology itself. The possibility of constructing what are effectively thinking machines, no matter how long the level of thought, is certain to have a profound influence not only on science but on economics and social life."

10. Radovan, Richta, *et al., Civilization at the Crossroads* (originally published in Prague, Czechoslovakia, 1967) by the *Australian Review,* published in English, Sydney, Australia, 1969, at 5.

11. *Ibid.,* at 9.

12. C. Vincent, W. Grossin, *L'en, et de l'Automotisation,* Paris, 1958, at 26, cited in *Ibid.,* at 10.

13. Karl Marx, *Grundrisse der Kritik der Politischen Okonomie,* Verlag für Fremdsprachige Literatur, Moskau, 1939, at 592–597.

14. *Ibid.*

15. Karl Marx, *supra* note 3 at 486.

16. In contrast to the view presented here, Herbert Marcuse suggests that automation *itself* alters the social relations of capitalist production because it "seems to alter qualitatively the relation between dead and living labor; it tends toward the point where productivity is determined 'by the machines, and not by the individual output' . . ." *See* his, *One-Dimensional Man, The Ideology of Industrial Society,* Sphere Books, Ltd., Great Britain, 1964, at 35–45. This is the basis for his conclusion that the working class is no longer the principal agent of revolutionary change in advanced capitalist society.

17. V. I. Lenin, *On the Material and Technical Basis of Communism,* Novosti Press Agency Publishing House, Moscow, 1969, at 37.

18. Jay M. Gould, *The Technical Elite,* Augustus M. Kelley, Publisher, New York, 1966, at 33.

19. J. M. Budish, *The Changing Structure of the Working Class,* International Publishers, New York, 1962, at 32.

20. Karl Marx, *supra* note 3 at 488.

21. Leland L. Medsker, *The Junior College*, McGraw-Hill Book Co., New York, 1960, at v.

22. William J. David, *The Impact of Junior Colleges on Engineering Education in the United States*, College of Engineering, Wayne State University, Detroit, Michigan, August, 1969 (mimeographed).

23. This view of the interpenetration of base and superstructure is *not* in contradistinction to the classical Marxist view of the relationship between the two. That is, that events in the superstructure are "determined in the last instance" by the economic base. For within this classical Marxist view is contained two essential elements: (1) there is a "relative autonomy" of the superstructure with respect to the base; (2) there is "reciprocal action" of the superstructure on the base. *See,* Louis Althusser, *Lenin and Philosophy*, and other essays, New Left Books, London, 1971. From our point of view it is precisely the revolution in the modes of production within the economic base, which has occasioned this change in the relationship between the university and the production process.

4   THE IDEOLOGICAL FUNCTIONS OF THE UNIVERSITY

1. Ernest Mandel, *Marxist Economic Theory*, Volume I, Monthly Review Press, New York, 1970, at 15.

2. Herbert Aptheker, "Lenin, Science and Revolution," *Political Affairs*, April, 1970, at 58 (Vol. XLIX, No. 4.).

3. Herbert Marcuse, *One Dimensional Man, The Ideology of Industrial Society*, Sphere Books, Ltd., Great Britain, at 27.

4. P. W. Bridgman, *The Logic of Modern Physics*, New York, MacMillan Co., 1928, at 5. In fairness to Bridgman it should be noted that in later writings he was far less rigid in his view of operationalism as an all-inclusive system of thought. In this connection a useful book is: A. Cornelius Benjamin, *Operationism*, Charles C. Thomas, Publisher, Springfield, Illinois, 1915. Benjamin for example, offers the following quotations to show Bridgman's modifications in his view:

    (1) "The Concept is synonymous with the corresponding set of operations" (1927);

    (2) "Meaning . . . is to be sought in operations" (1934);

    (3) Operations are a "necessary" but not a "sufficient" condition for the determination of meanings (1938);

    (4) "The operational aspect is not by any means the only aspect of meanings" (1952).

5. *Ibid.*, at 10.

6. *Ibid.*, at 30.

7. Abraham Kaplan, "The Travesty of the Philosophers," *Change,* January-February, 1970, at 14.

8. Herbert Marcuse, *supra* note 3 at 28.

9. Louis Kampf, "The Scandal of Literary Scholarship," in Theodore Roszak, editor, *The Dissenting Academy,* Pantheon Books, a division of Random House, New York, 1967, at 51.

10. Sumner M. Rosen, "Keynes Without Gadflies," in *Ibid.,* at 88–89.

11. Melville J. Ulmer, "Economics on the New Left," New Republic, December, 26, 1970, at 13.

12. Robert Engler, "Social Science and Social Consciousness," in Theodore Roszak, *supra,* note 9 at 194. This theme is also central to C. Wright Mills, *The Sociological Imagination,* Oxford University Press, New York, 1959, and it also appears in Alvin W. Gouldner, *The Coming Crisis of Western Sociology,* Basic Books, Inc., New York, 1970.

13. Office of External Research, U.S. Department of State, *Center of Foreign Affairs Research, A Directory,* Washington, D.C., 1968, at viii.

14. *Ibid.,* at ix.

15. *Ibid.,* at 92.

16. *Ibid.,* at 65.

17. Berkeley Rice, "The Cold War College Think Tanks," *Washington Monthly,* June, 1969, at 24.

18. American Institute for Research, *Counter-Insurgency in Thailand: The Impact of Economic, Social and Political Action Programs,* Pittsburgh, Pennsylvania, December, 1967, at 1, published in *The Student Mobilizer,* Volume 3, Number 4, April 2, 1970, by the Student Mobilization Committee to End the War in Vietnam, Washington, D.C.

19. *Ibid.,* at 2.

20. *Ibid.,* at 24, 25, and 26.

21. *Ibid.,* at 7.

22. Eric R. Wolf and Joseph G. Jorgensen, "Anthropology on the Warpath in Thailand," *New York Review of Books,* November 19, 1970, at 26.

23. *Ibid.*

24. American Institute for Research, *supra* note 18 at 34.

25. Center for Research and Advanced Studies, *Bulletin,* Volume V, No. 14, March 8, 1971, San Jose State College, at 3.

26. Howard Zinn, *The Politics of History,* Beacon Press, Boston, 1970, at 165.

27. George Jackson, *Soledad Brother,* Bantam Books, New York, 1970, at 29–30.

28. Obtained from the personal notes of Jessica Mitford, who had just completed research for her article, "Kind and Usual Punishment in California," *The Atlantic*, March, 1971.

29. James V. McConnell, "Criminals Can Be Brainwashed," *Psychology Today*, April, 1970, Vol. 3, No. 11 at 14–18, 74.

30. Herbert Marcuse, *Essay on Liberation*, Beacon Press, Boston, 1970, at 75.

31. Theodore R. Sarbin, "The Myth of the Criminal Type," Monday Evening Papers #18, Center for Advanced Studies, Weslyan University, 1969, 31 p.

32. Herbert L. Packer, "Crimes of Progress," *New York Review of Books*, October 23, 1969, at 17.

33. Edward C. Banfield, *The Unheavenly City: The Nature and Future of Our Urban Crisis*, Little, Brown, Boston, 1970, at 53, 62, 112, 163 and 211.

34. *Ibid.*, at 245–246.

35. Herbert Marcuse, *et al.*, *A Critique of Pure Tolerance*, Beacon Press, Boston, 1969, at 96.

36. This incident is reported by Kathleen Gough in her essay, "World Revolution and The Science of Man," in *The Dissenting Academy*, edited by Theodore Roszak, Pantheon Books, A Division of Random House, New York, 1967, at 137.

37. Franz Marek, *Philosophy of World Revolution*, International Publishers, New York, 1969, at 105.

5 THE STATE AND THE UNIVERSITY

1. Robert Paul Wolff, *The Ideal of the University*, Beacon Press, Boston, 1969, at 29.

2. V. I. Lenin, *The State and Revolution*, International Publishers, New York, 1968, at 9.

3. Karl Marx, *Capital*, Volume III, International Publishers, New York, 1967, at 376.

4. Frederick Engels, *Socialism: Utopian and Scientific*, International Publishers, New York, 1935, at 66–67.

5. This observation is made from a different vantage point by Walter Ulbricht, *The Significance and Vital Force of the Teachings of Karl Marx for our Era*, Berlin, 2 May 1968, at 47:

"Above all, however, it must be said that the entire living conditions of the working people in the capitalist countries are no longer *determined* by a boom-crisis cycle, but to an increasing extent by the effects of the scientific-technical revolution . . ."

6. Frederick Engels, *supra* note 4 at 59.

7. David Horowitz, "Sinews of Empire," *Ramparts,* October, 1969, at 33.

8. Institute for Defense Analysis, *Task Force Report on Science and Technology,* Washington, D.C., 1967, at 24.

9. John Weiss, "The University as a Corporation," *New University Thought,* Summer, 1965, at 41.

10. A. Hunter Dupree, *Science in the Federal Government,* Harvard University Press, Cambridge, Mass., 1957, at 7.

11. Frederick Rudolph, *The American College and University: A History,* Vintage Books, Random House, New York, 1962, at 232.

12. *Campus Report,* A Weekly Publication for Stanford University Faculty and Staff, Volume II, No. 24, April 1, 1970, at 2. See Also Alan Wolfe, "The Ph.D. Hard Times on Campus," *The Nation,* May 25, 1970, p. 623. According to Wolfe the crisis of overproduction has been developing for some time:

"One aspect of [it] is that doctoral output has been increasing more rapidly than faculty positions. Between 1940 and 1964 the number of faculty positions rose enormously—from 146,929 to 494,514, an increase of 337 percent. But in the same period the number of doctoral graduates increased 441 percent, from 3,290 a year to 14,490. Roughly four new Ph.D.'s were granted for every three new positions available."

13. Philip M. Boffey, "Budget Paradox: Spending Holds Even, Yet Researchers are Hurt," *Science,* Volume 162, October 18, 1968, at 340.

14. Mark W. Oberle, "Campus Computers: Federal Budget Cuts Hit University Center," *Science,* Volume 165, September 26, 1969, at 1337.

15. George Pake, "Basic Research and Financial Crisis in the Universities," *Science,* Volume 157, August 4, 1967, at 517.

16. See, for example: Philip M. Boffey, "Budget Trauma: NSF Funds Run Dry at University of Massachusetts," *Science,* Volume 162, November 15, 1968, at 776–779; Luther J. Carter, "Mathematics More Funds Urged for Science's 'Leading Wedge,' " *Science,* Volume 162, November 22, 1968, at 883; Joseph P. Martino, "Science and Society in Equilibrium," *Science,* Volume 165, August 22, 1969, at 769–772.

17. The emphasis on military priorities has repercussions in particular areas of scientific inquiry. See, for example, Tom Alexander, "The Hot New Promise of Thermonuclear Power," *Fortune,* June, 1970, at 95, Alexander discusses the problems and progress in the field of controlled thermonuclear fusion. While there is research going on in the United States, Alexander credits Soviet science with most of the major breakthroughs in this area. This is undoubtedly due, at least in part, to the allocation of greater resources, a reflection of Soviet

research priorities. The significance of controlled thermonuclear fusion is in its applicability as a safe, clean, plentiful, and relatively inexpensive source of energy. Alexander writes:

"The best index of a nation's living standard is the average amount of energy at the disposal of each citizen. Energy underlies most of the necessities: it is needed to produce fertilizers, extract materials, distribute goods, dispose of wastes, and supply warmth, among other things. But assuming that populations and living standards around the world will generally increase, future societies appear headed for energy starvation if they rely on present energy sources . . . Two methods of energy conversion should become available late in this century for averting at least this particular crunch. The closest to hand is the fast-breeder fission reactor, the technical and economic feasibility of which seem assured. The other, and potentially far better, is controlled thermonuclear fusion . . ."

18. *Manpower Comments,* Scientific Engineering Technical, Washington, D.C., Volume 6, No. 10, November, 1969, at 2.

19. *Ibid.* at 3.

20. *Ibid.* at 3.

21. Karl Hufbauer, *et al.,* "A Brief Critique of the Master Plan for Higher Education in California," New University Conference, Irvine Campus, University of California (mimeographed), March, 1970, at 1.

22. *Ibid.* at 2.

23. *A Master Plan for Higher Education in California* 1960–1975, Prepared for the Liaison Committee of the State Board of Education and the Regents of the University of California, Berkeley and Sacramento, February, 1960, at 2. Most states eventually adopted master plans for higher education. A similar institutionalization of class and racial discrimination may be found in Maryland. See, for example, the fine article by Paul Lauter and Florence Howe, "How the School System is Rigged for Failure," *New York Review of Books,* June 18, 1970, Volume XIV, No. 12 at 14–21.

24. *Ibid.* at 2–3.

25. *Ibid.* at 3.

26. Jess Unruh Report, *The Challenge of Achievement,* A Report on Public and Private Higher Education in California to the Joint Committee on Higher Education of the California Legislature, 1969, at 81.

27. Karl Hufbauer, *et al., supra* note 21 at 2.

28. *Ibid.* at 3.

29. Arthur G. Coons, *Crisis in California Higher Education,* The Ward Ritchie Press, Los Angeles, 1968, at 149.

6 ALIENATION

1. Karl Marx, *Capital,* Volume II, International Publishers, New York, 1967, at 219.

2.᾿ Karl Marx and Frederick Engels, *The Communist Manifesto,* International Publishers, New York, 1962, at 15.

3. In exploring this crisis of overproduction studies are undertaken to determine the supply, demand and utilization of scientists and engineers. Some of these reports are particularly illustrative of their commodity-status. See John D. Alden, "Engineering Job Prospects for 1970," *Manpower Comments,* Scientific-Engineering Technical, April, 1970, Volume 7, No. 4 at 4–5:

"To summarize, most economists are predicting a further business slowdown, even a recession. This will undoubtedly curb the rapid expansion of engineering jobs, at least temporarily. The impact will, however, be cushioned by the following built-in factors:

Continued long-range growth in the need for engineers due to irreversible factors in our technological society. Decline in manpower demand in one specialized field tends to be offset by increased emphasis in others, and new engineering graduates can be used quite flexibly outside their primary disciplines.

The requirement of a large percentage of new graduates just to replace deaths and retirements in a profession now numbering close to a million engineers.

A backlog of engineering jobs that have had to be filled by non-graduates over the last 20 years.

Substantial current immigration, which can be slowed down quickly whenever manpower surpluses develop in engineering fields.

A strong and growing demand for engineering graduates to fill non-engineering jobs.

An unusually large reduction in the supply of new graduates available for civilian employment because of the new random draft procedures.

All in all, then, I am inclined to believe that there will be less of a crisis in the engineering job hunt this year than might be assumed from some of the alarmist stories being repeated in the public press."

4. Karl Marx and Frederick Engels, *The German Ideology,* International Publishers, New York, 1969, at 7. The anthropological basis for this view of man was, of course, developed by Engels at length in *Origins of the Family, Private Property and the State,* International Publishers, New York. Here Engels argued that the use of tools (i.e., production) made possible by the combination in man of the opposable thumb and his cranial capacity, was the critical factor in man's separation from the rest of the animal kingdom.

5. Karl Marx, *Capital,* Volume I, International Publishers, New York, 1967, at 178.

6. Karl Marx and Frederick Engels, *supra* note 4 at 7.

7. Karl Marx, *supra* note 5 at 177.

8. Roger Garaudy, *Karl Marx: The Evolution of His Thought,* International Publishers, New York, 1967, at 61. Garaudy's discussion of alienation is brilliant, and was especially helpful in the preparation of this chapter.

9. Andre Ure, *Philosophie des manufactures ou economie industrielle,* Volume I, Chapter I, p. 34, cited by Karl Marx, *The Poverty of Philosophy,* Foreign Languages Publishing House, Moscow, Third Impression, at 136.

10. Karl Marx, *Economic and Philosophic Manuscripts* (1844), in Loyd D. Easton and Kurt H. Guddat, editors, *Writings of the Young Marx on Philosophy and Society,* Doubleday, New York, 1967, at 291.

11. In this connection consider the speech given by Mario Savio at the Berkeley campus of the University of California December 2, 1964, at the height of the Free Speech Movement: "There is a time when the operation of the machine becomes so odious, makes you so sick at heart that you cannot take part, you can't even tacitly take part. And you've got to put your body upon the gears, and upon the wheels and upon the levers and upon all the apparatus and you've got to make it stop. And you've got to indicate to the people who own it, and to the people who run it that unless you are free, their machine will be prevented from running at all."

12. See Clark Kerr, *The Uses of the University,* Harvard University Press, Cambridge, 1963. For a particularly satisfying rebuttal, see Robert Paul Wolff, *The Ideal of the University,* Chapter Three, "The University as a Social Service Station," Beacon Press, Boston, 1969.

13. Karl Marx, *supra,* note 10 at 292.

14. Judson Jerome, *Culture out of Anarchy, the Reconstruction of American Higher Learning,* Herder and Herder, New York, 1970, at xx.

15. Christian Bay, "Student Political Activism: Here To Stay?" (Presented to a Symposium on Committed and Alienated Youth, March 21, 1967, at the Annual Meeting of the American Orthopsychiatric Association in Washington, D.C.) at 6.

16. Alan Wolfe, "The Myth of the Free Scholar," *The Center Magazine,* July, 1969, at 74, 75.

17. Karl Marx, *supra,* note 10 at 290.

18. Robert Hodes, *Aims and Methods of Scientific Research,* published by the American Institute for Marxist Studies, New York, 1968,

at 8. Dr. Hodes based his own definition on that given by William Cecil Dampier-Wetham, *A History of Science and its Relation with Philosophy and Religion,* Cambridge University Press, 1943, p. XIII.

19. An interesting dimension in the Hodes paper is its insistence that: "At the heart of the scientific method lies observation. Once again, the popular concept of science (and, I might add, the concept of most scientists) is that scientific data result from experiment . . . Careful observation of natural phenomena is another way of securing serviceable facts of science. We need mention nothing more to prove this than to remind you that one of the truly great scientific theories of all time was elaborated without recourse to a single experiment. I refer here to Darwin's theory of evolution. Darwin observed nature, recorded his observations with meticulous care and astounding pre-science and thereby gained the raw material for his theory . . ." see *ibid.,* at 11, 15.

20. *Ibid.,* at 17.

21. Alfred Stern, "Science and the Philosopher," in Paul C. Obler and Herman A. Estrin, editors, *The New Scientist, Essays on the Methods and Values of Modern Science,* Doubleday, New York, 1962, at 286.

22. *Ibid.* at 286.

23. Karl Marx in a letter to Kugelman, 11 July 1868, quoted by Alfred Schmidt, *The Concept of Nature in Marx,* London, New Left Books, 1971, at 98.

24. Alfred Schmidt, *The Concept of Nature in Marx,* London, New Left Books, 1971, at 15.

25. *Ibid.* at 68.

26. T. B. Bottomore, trans., and ed., *Karl Marx, Selected Writings in Sociology and Social Philosophy,* New York, McGraw-Hill, 1964, at 73.

27. Carl Marzani, ed., *The Open Marxism of Antonio Gramsci,* Cameron Associates, New York, 1957, at 45.

28. Richard Lichtman, "The University: Mask for Privilege," *The Center* Magazine, January, 1968, Volume I, No. 2 at 7.

29. A striking example of this may be seen in the criticism of several scientists connected in various ways with the National Aeronautics and Space Administration; in particular, with the Apollo moon project. *See,* for example, the recent book by astronaut-scientist Brian O'Leary, *The Making of an Ex-Astronaut,* Houghton-Mifflin, New York, 1970, 243 pp.

30. Werner Heisenberg, "Uber den anschaulichen Inhalt der quantentheoretischen Kinematik and Mechanik," *Zeitschrift für Physik,* Vol. 43, Berlin, 1927, p. 197, cited by Alfred Stern, *supra,* note 19 at 294.

31. Alfred Stern, *supra*, note 21 at 293.

32. Adolph Baker, *Modern Physics and Anti-physics*, Addison-Wesley Publishing Co., Reading, Massachusetts, 1970, at 203, 204, 208.

33. Alfred Stern, *supra*, note 21 at 287.

34. Abraham Kaplan, "The Travesty of the Philosophers," *Change*, January-February, 1970, at 14.

35. *Manpower Comments*, Scientific and Engineering Technical, Washington, D.C., Volume 7, Number 2, February, 1970, at 6–7.

36. Portions of a speech delivered on May 4, 1969, by Professor Barry Commoner during a teach-in at Washington University, St. Louis, Missouri.

37. Robert S. Lynd, *Knowledge For What? The Place of the Social Science in American Culture*, Grove Press, New York, 1964 (originally published in 1939 by Princeton University Press) 182.

38. *Ibid.* at 183.

7 THE MARXIST PHILOSOPHY

1. V. I. Lenin, *Materialism and Empirio-Criticism*, International Publishers, New York, 1970 (original-1908) at 159–160.

2. David Bohm, *Causality and Chance in Modern Physics*, Harper Torchbacks, New York, 1957, at 2, 23.

3. J. D. Bernal, *Science in History*, Hawthorn Books, Inc., New York, 1965, at 949.

4. Frederick Engels, *Dialectics of Nature* (1892) pp. 183 f., cited by Howard Selsam & Harry Martel, editors, *Reader in Marxist Philosophy*, International Publishers, New York, 1963, at 170.

5. Umberto Cerroni, "Socialist Humanism and Science," in *Socialist Humanism*, edited by Erich Fromm, Doubleday, Anchor Books Edition, 1966, at 136.

6. Frederick Engels, *Anti-Duhring, Herr Eugan Duhring's Revolution in Science*, Foreign Languages Publishing House, Moscow, 1959, at 367.

7. Frederick Engels, Letter to Franz Mehring, July 14, 1893, in *Selected Correspondence of Karl Marx and Frederick Engels*, (1846–1895), International Publishers, New York, 1942, at 512.

8. Georg Lukacs, *Lenin: A Study on the Unity of his Thought*, first published by Verlag der Arbeiterbuchhandlung, Vienna, 1924, this translation published by New Left Books, 1970, London, England, at 43.

9. Roger Garaudy, *Karl Marx: The Evolution of His Thought*, International Publishers, New York, 1967, at 57.

10. Caleb Foote, et. al., *The Culture of the University: Governance*

and Education, Report of the Study Commission on University Governance, published by the *Daily Californian,* University of California, Berkeley, 1968, at 7.

8 NOTES ON THE REBELLION

1. Gil Green, *The New Radicalism: Anarchist or Marxist?,* International Publishers, New York, 1971, at 148.
2. Details on this appeared in *Academe,* publication of the American Association of University Professors, Volume 5, Number 1, February, 1971, at 1.
3. Jeffrey Harrison, "Student Bargaining," *The New Republic,* November 21, 1970, at 10–11.
4. Karl Marx and Frederick Engels, *The Communist Manifesto,* International Publishers, New York, 1962, at 17.
5. V. I. Lenin, *What Is To Be Done?,* International Publishers, New York, 1969, at 31.
6. Karl Marx and Frederick Engels, *The German Ideology,* International Publishers, New York, second printing, 1960, at 21.

9 PROBLEMS OF ACADEMIC FREEDOM

1. Sheldon S. Wolin and John H. Schaar, "Is a New Politics Possible?" *New York Review of Books,* September 3, 1970, Volume XV, Number 4, at 3.
2. *Ibid.* at 3.
3. American Association of University Professors, "The 1915 Declaration of Principles," in Louis Joughin, editor, *Academic Freedom and Tenure,* A Handbook of the American Association of University Professors, University of Wisconsin Press, 1969 edition, at 166.
4. The crisis in defining the principles of academic freedom is recognized by many academicians. Wolin and Schaar suggest it in the above cited article (*supra,* note 1). See also Walter P. Metzger, "Academic Freedom, in Delocalized Academic Institutions," in *Dimensions of Academic Freedom,* University of Illinois Press, Urbana, Illinois, 1969, at 1–33. Metzger writes:
The gist of the argument that follows is that the theory of academic freedom as it has been articulated in this country has become, in critical respects, outmoded . . . as a mode of analysis and advice concerning the realities of social power . . . I believe the inherited canon has, to a large extent, outlived its day. . . .
5. Fritz Machlup, "On Some Misconceptions Concerning Academic Freedom," in Louis Joughin, editor, *Academic Freedom and*

Tenure, A Handbook of the American Association of University Professors, University of Wisconsin Press, 1969, at 169.

6. American Association of University Professors, "The 1915 Declaration of Principles," *supra,* note 3 at 169.

7. *Ibid.,* at 169.

8. Walter P. Metzger, *Academic Freedom in the Age of the University,* Columbia University Press, New York, 1964, at 112.

9. American Association of University Professors, "The 1915 Declaration of Principles," *supra,* note 3 at 157–158.

10. Walter P. Metzger, *Academic Freedom in the Age of the University, supra,* note 8 at 114–115.

11. Fritz Machlup, "On Some Misconceptions Concerning Academic Freedom," *supra,* note 5 at 179.

12. Frederick Rudolph, *The American College and University,* Vintage Books, A Division of Random House, New York, 1962, at 411.

13. *Ibid.,* at 411.

14. See, for example, Ralph Fuchs, "Academic Freedom—Its Basic Philosophy, Function and History," in Louis Joughin, editor, *Academic Freedom and Tenure,* Handbook of the American Association of University Professors, University of Wisconsin Press, 1969, at 243.

15. Cited by Herbert Aptheker in his essay "Communism and Truth: A Reply to Sidney Hook," in his book *The Era of McCarthyism,* Marzani & Munsell, New York, 1955, at 89.

16. Robert Paul Wolff, *The Poverty of Liberalism,* Beacon Press, Boston, 1968, at 15 and 17.

17. V. I. Lenin, *What Is To Be Done?,* International Publishers, New York, 1969, at 11.

18. See, for example, the communication from J. D. Human, Professor of Law, State University of New York at Buffalo in the *New Republic,* October 25, 1969, at 30–31. Also, a particularly devastating critique of Jensen is "Intelligence and Race" by Walter F. Bodmer and Luigi Luca Cavalli-Sforza, (both geneticists) in *Scientific America,* Vol. 223, Number 4, October, 1970, pp. 19–29.

19. Andrew M. Greeley, "Malice in Wonderland: Misperceptions of the Academic Elite," *Change,* The Magazine of Higher Education, September-October 1970, at 34.

20. Christian Bay, "Political and Apolitical Students: Facts in Search of Theory," delivered at the annual meeting of the Society for the Psychological Study of Social Issues, Washington, D.C., September 2, 1966.

21. Herbert Aptheker, "The United States: Decay and Rebirth," *International Affairs,* Moscow, No. 10, October, 1969, at 9.

22. Alexander Mitscherlich, *et al., Doctors of Infamy: The Story of the Nazi Medical Crimes,* Henry Schuman Publishers, New York, 1949. Dr. Andrew C. Ivy wrote the preface.

23. Henry Steele Commager, "The University as Employment Agency," *New Republic,* February 24, 1968, at 25.

10   THE RADICAL RECONSTRUCTION OF HIGHER LEARNING

1. *Daily Californian,* student newspaper published at the Berkeley campus of the University of California, Tuesday, March 4, 1969, Volume 201, No. 43, at 7.

2. *Ibid.,* at 7.

3. *Ibid.,* at 7.

4. *Ibid.,* at 10.

5. Robert Paul Wolff, *The Ideal of the University,* Beacon Press, Boston, 1969, at 92.

6. Barrington Moore, Jr., "On Rational Inquiry in Universities Today," *New York Review of Books,* April 23, 1970, Volume XIV, No. 8, at 35.

7. Sékou Touré, "A Dialectical Approach to Culture," *The Black Scholar,* November, 1969, at 3–18.

8. John Hurt Fisher, editor, *Publications of the Modern Languages Association of America,* September, 1970, Vol. 85, Number 4, at 654. The resolution reads: "Whereas the Spanish-speaking population of the Southwest and elsewhere has been deprived of its political and cultural self-determination ever since the Mexican American War when this territory was conquered. Whereas the agreements subscribed by the U.S. Government in the signing of the Guadalupe-Hidalgo Treaty of 1848 with Mexico regarding the equal treatment of Mexican citizens, their property, and language have been broken. Whereas the farm and city workers, women and students of this community of peoples have been subjected to a continuous history of repression at the hands of their conquerors. Whereas the historical struggles and the rich cultural heritage of this Indo-Hispano nation have been concealed from the bulk of American citizens: *Be it Resolved* that as an initial step to remedy this injustice, this body of scholars and students of language and literature (MLA) give moral and financial support: (1) to the establishment of bilingual and bicultural courses and programs currently developing into Chicano or La Raza Studies; (2) to the hiring of Chicano administrators, faculty, and staff to implement these programs (as well as other departments); (3) to the increased enrollment of Chicano and Latino students in numbers at least equal to their percentage in the population. *Be it further resolved* that all

teachers presently engaged in the teaching of the language and literature of the Hispanic peoples in Spanish-speaking areas in the U.S.A.
make use of and/or help develop materials and the understanding
necessary to bring to fruition the potential social wealth of this bilingual and bicultural forgotten American population."

9. Karl Marx, *Economic and Philosophic Manuscripts* (1844), in
Loyd D. Easton and Kurt H. Guddat, editors, *Writings of the Young
Marx on Philosophy and Society,* Doubleday, New York, 1967, at 299.

10. Bernard Murchland, "Education Test: Relevant to What?" the
Wall Street Journal, Thursday, June 4, 1970. (The article originally
appeared in the April, 1970, issue of *Worldview Magazine,* monthly
journal of the Council on Religion and International Affairs. The
author is a member of the philosophy department of Ohio Wesleyan
University.)